To
Chris & Tom
Best Wishes
[signature]

"His Way Mine"

God has a place for every planned creation,
A path for every star to go.
He drew the course of every river's journey;
Now I know he has a way for me.

I place my life in the hands of God.
Those hands so scarred now outstretched for me.
Wherever it may be, over land, over sea,
May thy will sublime, O Thou God divine, be mine.

(Dick Baker)
Used by permission.

A Faith Journey
No Boundaries, No Conclusions

ROBERT L. MADDOX, JR

© 2018

Published in the United States by Nurturing Faith Inc., Macon GA,

www.nurturingfaith.net.

Library of Congress Cataloging-in-Publication Data is available.

ISBN 978-1-63528-045-6

Cover image by pixelparticle.

To Linda Maddox, children and grandchildren, nieces and nephews, and that great cloud of witnesses.

Special thanks to Ferew M. Haile for his invaluable technical assistance.

TABLE OF CONTENTS

CHAPTER ONE

Perspective

While I was working on this memoir, my mother died. Right before Christmas 2014 she took a bad fall in the care facility into which she had moved just a few months before her death. My brothers and I, along with our extended family, grieved but also had to celebrate. She lived 103 years, from 1911 until 2014. She was born in the Alabama town of Roanoke, not too far from the Georgia line, delivered by her Uncle Henry, the country doctor who still got about in a horse-drawn buggy.

She remembered the first airplane that flew over her town; it nearly killed her. At about five years old she had come down with the deadly flu that scourged the nation like medieval plagues. It seems that this phenomenal flying machine, as it zipped over the treetops, crashed out on the edge of town. Word of the incident flashed through the village with lightning speed even to my mother's sick bed. She bounced out of bed and raced to the site of the fallen plane, determined to see this newfangled wonder with her own eyes. My grandmother came screaming after her in a panic, lest the flagrant exposure kill Virginia, the only daughter in a family of four sons.

She survived the flu. She survived World War I. She survived the abandonment of the family by her ne'er-do-well father. She finished high school—the first in her family to do so—and later helped her younger brother get his diploma. Not daunted by the Great Depression, she got a decent job in Atlanta, where she met and married the love of her life, my father. She survived World War II, which was made all the more personal to her by the four tumultuous years living in Portsmouth and Norfolk, Virginia, where my father worked 24/7 building ships. Twin sons, totally unexpected in those pre-sonogram days, came six weeks early. Needing a serious operation, she left her four young sons with a friend and rode the ferry and bus to the hospital because my father could not leave his critical work to drive her to the surgery. Back home in Georgia after the war, she survived three years in a country farmhouse on a dirt road—at first with no indoor toilet and no telephone—warmed by a huge pot-bellied, coal-fired heater and never enough water in the well.

My father died far too early from neglected cancer, and she survived. She survived exponentially advancing technology that swirled around her but left her largely unfazed. She did not resist the changes. She simply did not want all that stuff. A good car she drove for twenty years and color television met her needs. Though a whiz with a manual typewriter, she blithely skipped computers and cell phones. When her new hearing aids quit working, she put them in the dresser drawer, never bothering to get someone to help her change the batteries. She always dressed to the nines. She made weekly trips to the beauty shop until almost the day of that fatal fall. Church was always on the schedule. Bottom line: she made her own way until well into that fateful 103rd year. We never had to second-guess her. If she wanted to go with us, she put on her coat and draped the ubiquitous purse over her "ahm" (that's South Georgia speak for *arm*). Or she would say, "No, you all go ahead. I'm fine here," and we would leave.

As she approached birthday 103, she made two announcements to us. By then living across the lane from one of my brothers in the hills of Arkansas, she decided it would be too complicated and costly to have her body transported to Georgia when she died to be buried next to my father. She would be cremated. And that's what we did. She also decided she needed to move into the nearby care facility because her legs were giving way and she kept falling. And that's what happened.

I recall this remarkable life because she lived through the most remarkable, great, and terrible century in the long history of the human race. Her century paralleled, encapsulated this epic roaring hundred years. Trying to get inside her century provides something of a vantage point for me to grapple with my own years. She experienced just about every trauma of any person I know. You name it; she could match it, although she would never say, "You don't know anything. Let me tell you what happened to me."

To a degree that only of late has dawned on me, both my parents simply bowed their backs and moved on. With an almost total lack of looking back, they rounded the next bend in the road, climbed the next hill. Misfortune hurt but did not stop them. Both had a significant if not a particularly reflective Baptist faith. Their straightforward relationship with God served as a bulwark against religious fads that crop up all the time. The "faith once received" sufficed. In it all Mother blessed and loved us completely, though she generally avoided profound emotional connection, or so it appeared to me. She fully understood our sins and foibles. Like the mother hen in the barnyard, she kept us all under her wings, if somewhat loosely. As a way to demonstrate her care for the brood, again almost to her last days, she wrote in a completely legible hand, all the children, spouses (even those now outside the immediate circle by divorce), grandchildren, and great-grandchildren a birthday "caad" (that's South Georgia for *card*).

My parents bequeathed to me a legacy of their own equanimity, a capacity to deal with what happens. Unlike them, however, I have a generous measure of curiosity made invigorating and less daunting by their measure of existential security to push ahead into the new century that beckons. In language borrowed from English theologian Don Cupitt, I have cast off from familiar moorings and am finding the exhilaration of "sailing on the sea of faith." Come sail with me.

My parents left no money to any of us. They did bequeath to me a place to stand to make my own life and carve out my own approach to life and faithing. On the heels of their century, I pick up the mantle in the latter days of my own rapidly passing time. Celebrate with me a coming-of-age faith perspective that offers a place to stand amidst exhilarating, wide-open emotional and spiritual vistas. Take a deep breath as we move into a grand world with no periods, replete with beckoning commas. Risky, even scary—but my! —the liberation, promise and hope!

And from here on through this highly selective, rather free-floating faithing memoir, remember I have not been a stand-alone pilgrim on this journey. It's my journey traversed in the company of some astounding people. Talk about evolving, collaborative faith; I am the poster-child for that exciting, roiling, and compelling adventure.

I am one of those older southern white guys who grew up in a time falsely remembered as dependable from one day to the next. I am also a white guy who, from a fairly early age, had the gnawing suspicion that things were not as nailed down as they appeared. I just did not know what I did not know. A myriad of swirling energies kept me near the edge of what I knew not. Gratefully, some key people with generative ideas provided beacons to keep me from getting totally blown away. A wise preacher, his name long gone, said of an old sailor, "I don't know much about the wind, but I know how to set my sails." Those manifold winds, many of which I could not fathom, blew sufficiently to fill my sails to keep me moving. Go with me to our own twenty-first-century iteration of Ithaka.

> Have Ithaka always in your mind.
> Your arrival there is what you are destined for.
> But don't in the least hurry the journey.
> Better it last for years,
> so that when you reach the island you are old,
> rich with all you have gained on the way,
> not expecting Ithaka to give you wealth.
> Ithaka gave you a splendid journey.
> Without her you would not have set out.
> She hasn't anything else to give you.
>
> And if you find her poor, Ithaka hasn't deceived you.
> So wise you have become, of such experience,
> that already you'll have understood what these Ithakas mean.[1]
>
> From " Ithaka" by C.P. Cavafy

CHAPTER TWO

My Faithing

Some linguistic experts have lamented that in the English language we lack a verb form for *faith*. Someone proposed *faithing* as a verb form. I will adopt that approach and say I have been and remain on a "faithing" journey. *Faithing* connotes an active mindset; it has to do with praxis (I hope this is not too awkward). So I want to talk about my personal faithing journey as I turn the corner at age eighty.

As this writing progressed, I finally got around to asking myself what I mean by *faithing*. A key question for me to confront, never too late. In the middle of the night recently, the Muse paid me a visit. Rather than risk waiting until morning to write down what she gave me, I pulled myself out of sleep, grabbed my handy phone, and made notes. For me faithing is hope, confidence, commitment, trust, praxis. These are tethered to, embraced by, infused with a sense of providence, the holy, cosmic order (Rom 8:28), the way it should be. There's more for me. I also deeply recognize that my best efforts are only approximations.

I will talk about faithing as poetry and imagination. Not precise. Not given to neat definitions. As this book unfolded over several years, I was pushed back to halcyon, theologically simpler days before church and denominational life became so full of silly conflicts that diminished delight. I will reflect on this more, but I recall my freshman year Friday night Singspirations in the beautiful drawing room on the campus union building at Baylor University. Students went out into the city to do a variety of mission endeavors, especially in the more hard-pressed parts of Waco. Afterward, we would gather for an hour or so singing campfire-like, inspirational songs. My all-time favorite was Baylor's own Dick Baker's "His Way Mine." The enchanting song invited us to seek the will of God for our lives, to place ourselves in the "outreached hands" of God as the way to abundant living. With all my heart I wanted that connection. I did not parse the words. At that teenage time in my developing life, I took the words literally. God—out there, up there—had his wonderful eyes on me, sketching out a plan for me, eighteen-year-old Bob Maddox, in the same way he had set the stars in motion and laid out the rivers' courses. The song became all the more important when the composer himself visited the campus and played and sang his music for us. When Linda and I married in 1959, Ann Herring sang "His Way Mine" as part of the ceremony. The song has stayed with Linda and me.

I am glad to say I have grown with the song. In an energizing and fulfilling evolution I now understand the song more clearly through the refracted lens of poetry and imagination. In a richer way the words get down inside me, offering the opportunity to open myself to all manner of growth angles that enhance my faithing journey into the beckoning realms of life-framing poetry and imagination.

So now I talk about my faithing journey in a confessional motif rather than a doctrinal or formalistic framework. I do not hesitate to say "I"—risky but honest for me. When all's said and done, what matters is what makes sense to the individual (in this case to me). It took me some time to come to this rather unsettling personal moment, to come of age at eighty...maybe. A friend of decades sent me some words by which he lives, "Now I become myself."

I have traveled a long, exciting road. When Will, my oldest grandson (now twenty-six), wrote a fifth-grade essay about me, he began by saying, "My grandfather has lived a very interesting life." I have his essay framed and on my bookcase. I agree with Will. We'll get to the details in a bit. But as we start out together, just know that all in all I am satisfied with and grateful for the road I have traveled. Do I have regrets? Yes! Would I do some (many) things differently? Of course. But all in all it's been quite a trip. And I am quick to confess it remains quite the trip. No periods, only commas. So far, so good! I wish the same for you.

I am not promoting my way for you over other ways you might choose— though when we are through reading these pages together, I can hope you will chart your own way more clearly, with more security, less anxiety, finding a firmer place to stand despite the ever-shifting sands of daily life. To be real, life and its connecting *faithing* have to be our own—faithing toward freedom.

My Buddhist friends have a way of saying they are finding the right way. That does not mean their right way is right for everyone. That's not the Buddhist way, nor is it the way of Jesus. "Right way" connotes what fits for you. This present right way fits for me. When you try on a new coat or a new pair of gloves or shoes, you know when they fit. They just feel right for you. That's the right way for me at this point. Do you wear the same coat year round? The same pair of gloves in winter and shoes in summer? Of course not. The coat wears out. The gloves get holes in the fingers; the soles of the shoes get thin. Your size and needs change, so you go for another coat or gloves or shoes. It works for me at eighty: fits for the season, then change.

Hey, you might say, that's sort of wishy-washy isn't it? Surely my way is more dependable than that! Refocus a bit: The given is clothes. You take your clothes off to take a bath, but generally speaking you need clothes on your body. Fashions change with the times. The weight of the garment varies with the season. But the need for clothing remains. Some sense of fit is essential. The clothes can change, but the need for them remains a constant.

What wears well and fits your lifestyle when you are a teenager could, most likely, be totally out of place when you get your first big job at the bank or the law office or the police force. I have old pictures of myself all decked out in polyester suits with my hair down over my ears. Those suits were nifty in the 1960s but laughable in these days. Sad to say, I know far too many people who wear the same spiritual psyche today as adults—even older adults—that they wore as teenagers or twenty-year-olds. An old saw comes to mind: The daughter notices that her mother always cuts off the end of the ham before she puts it in the pan to bake. Finally, as the daughter prepares to cook her own ham, she asks her mother, "Why do you cut the end of the ham off before you cook it?" Rather stunned by the question, with a look on her face that says she never asked herself that question, she responds, "Well, my mother always cut off the end of the ham. Let's ask her the next time she's here." The grandmother replied when queried about the ham cutting, "My baking pan was too small to hold the entire ham. Times were hard. Rather than buy a larger pan, I just cut off the end of the ham." Why do you and I do it, think it the same way all the time?

My "myness" is always mine, especially if I am trying to be honest with myself. But myness changes with time and circumstances. If your myness never changes, you're stuck in a rather grinding, unproductive rut. If that's your choice, go for it. It's just not my way.

I take personal responsibility for my way at eighty. If I am on a wrong track, it's my track I have chosen. Or maybe I should say the way I am still choosing. I am quick to say that where I am at this point in life surely does seem to fit me to a T. If I am granted a few more years, will I still be where I am today? Probably not, surely not entirely. I will still be me. I will still need love, affirmation, encouragement from some key folks in my life. I will still lay claim to a basic, existential acceptance of my overall life. But working solutions to life's complexities, changes, sudden turns in the road will push me to maneuver through whatever life deals out.

So this is my way. I do not share Frank Sinatra's view that it's my way or the highway. But it is my way. I welcome you to sort through your own framing ideas. Along the way take that fateful deep breath and begin to chart your way. Much good, solid help is readily available to keep you from getting too far off track too soon. Come on. It's a great adventure. Remember it was none other than Jesus himself who offered us an abundant life (John 10:10).

CHAPTER THREE

Fellow Travelers

I am quick to say, again, I did not get here by myself. "No man is an island," they say. Or "it takes a village." I am me. Myness is mine. Yet I am anything but a monad. Look at the dedication of the book: "To Linda and that great cloud of witnesses."

It was indeed a salient day when I met Linda Cook of Thomaston, Georgia, in 1956. It was an even more stupendous day when we married in her hometown in 1959. Now headed toward sixty years together, I continue to live in and out of that framing, energizing, love-filled, ever-growing relationship. The day of our wedding, I celebrated her "indefatigable energy." I never spoke truer, more prescient words.

We are products of all that has gone on before us (note: this will be part of the recurring theme of this book). At the same time we are not irrevocably, everlastingly bound by that which has produced us.

As we move along in this effort, you will see me giving heartfelt credit to folks I can recall. Even as I write, people long forgotten pop into my head, emerge from the mists. Though I have given a sketch of my mother, I will talk more about my parents, especially my father, further in the narrative. They were solid parents, doing the very best they could for my three brothers and me. Perfect? No. But stand-up folks by all means.

Dorothy Holloway Cook—my late, great, wise, sensible mother-in-law—blessed and taught me as much basic practical theology and down-home ethics as anyone I have known. Her sagacity moved seamlessly from the Bible to Shakespeare to South Georgia proverbs. She never missed a beat with the right word at the right moment. I have been blessed by her.

Rev. Earle Stirewalt immersed me in the chilly baptismal waters in the indoor pool of the Lithonia Baptist Church in suburban Atlanta. A kind and gentle man who blessed me then as a thirteen-year-old and blesses me yet though I have not seen him in decades.

I remember Miss Ethel Jones, my Baptist Sunday school leader when I was about twelve years old. She was a grand, straight-laced, unmarried woman with definite ideas about Jesus and the church and what we ought to do. Even then I disagreed with some of what she said but to object openly never crossed my mind. She loved us kids and gave herself devotedly to us.

H. B. Simms led our all-boys teenage Sunday school class. For a living he taught high school history at an Atlanta-area high school. As much as any other person, he whetted my appetite for history as he expertly filled in some of the historical blanks in the Bible stories we ambled through in Sunday school.

Alonzo McDonald—a bright, eager cub reporter with an Atlanta newspaper—held our teenage Sunday school class spellbound as he regaled us with episodes from the streets of the city, especially nefarious nighttime deeds. I am not sure how much Bible we got, but he conveyed the unmistakable idea that church was not all dust from the long ago. From time to time I still encounter him, a man like others I have known who pushed against boundaries.

Mrs. Roy Sparks, the mother of the Sparks twins in our church, volunteered as the long-suffering leader of our Sunday evening youth sessions—Baptist Training Union, we called it in those long-ago days.

George Cowden—fresh out of the U.S. Air Force, a law student at Baylor University—became the leader of our campus-wide Baptist Student Union. I was elected president of the organization and worked with George for two years—first as a volunteer and then for one year after graduation as his paid assistant. What a man! With a quiet, reflective, far-reaching faith that permeated every ounce of his being, he influenced me and countless more Baylor Bears. He would offer wisdom, "Make a good ready; the world will wait." When Linda and I decided to marry, he said, "Bob and Linda, remember, it's the two of you against the world." Tragically, one of his sons happened to be in the Aurora, Colorado, movie theater with his teenage daughters the night of the horrible 2012 shooting. Gordon was killed in the massacre. I wrote George telling him how much he had meant to me and how I grieved at his loss. Unspeakable. And not long ago his beloved wife, Molly, succumbed to an extended illness.

Charles Welborn stands out as college church pastor beyond compare for me. Growing up, I had known a few ministers. A couple of them took up time with me, but none stirred and elevated heart and mind like Charles Welborn.

Across the years I would find an occasion to write him, telling him what he had done for a very green Baylor student. A few years ago I learned he was facing a serious illness. I tracked him down and called him one more time. We reminisced about the grand old days at Waco's Seventh and James Baptist Church on the Baylor campus. He died a short time later, a loss to me and many more.

Charles Rice came into my life—actually, into our family's life—during that pivotal summer of 1955 when the Maddox clan spent a week at Glorieta Baptist Assembly near Santa Fe, New Mexico. A brilliant teenager from California, he had a won a speaking contest sponsored by a Baptist organization and earned a trip to the assembly. He had several meals with us. When I learned that he and other young people on the support staff of the assembly were going to Baylor University, I decided that was the school for me. Charles had a profound influence on my student life and beyond, though I have not had any direct contact with him for decades. After completing all his various graduate degrees, he taught theology at a prestigious East Coast seminary.

I met Bill Rogers as he entered Baylor University in 1957, two years behind me. He remains one of those truly formative characters in my story. Unfailingly, he stays on the cutting edge, readily pointing me in fresh directions. We named our two sons after Bill. He is that standout friend and soulmate, though we see each other far too infrequently. Bill gave us a scare a few months ago as he faced a life-threatening illness. Love of a great wife, legions of friends, and an astounding medical team pulled him through.

June Powell and Madge Methvin in my first pastorate; Mattie Lou Strain and Frances Burton-Cochran of the Calhoun, Georgia church family; and neighbors Kyle and Vivian Smith graced me with their support and friendship. Later came Frank and Marge Harvey, the Mabry family, Tim and Amy Tutt, and on and on, a considerable legion of people who have made indelible impressions on me, shaping my faith, my world, in ways beyond words and recall. Myness reminds me then that I am the recipient of countless gifts of love and encouragement from the likes of George Gaston, Tony Martin, Mary Ann Wood, and Tommy McDearis to name a few.

For Linda and me and our family, Jimmy and Rosalynn Carter have affirmed and encouraged us over the past fifty years, especially since President Carter's election in 1976. Experiences at the Carter Center in Atlanta and with his church in Plains, Georgia, enrich Linda and me. We have been able to maintain cordial friendships with members of the Carters' immediate family and White House staff. I will return often to him and his ongoing influence on our world and me even down to this day.

The inimitable Rev. Gordon Cosby looms large, though I had minimal face-to-face contact with him. I will talk more fully about him further on, remembering that his pervasive influence runs through much of my faithing journey, beginning in the early 1970s. He died at age ninety-five in 2013. He was a Jesus man with every fiber of his Virginia-born body. Inclusive, a critic of anyone in power who would marginalize the least of these, a person of deep spirit with prayer as daily companion. Animated by a reverential regard for Scripture, Gordon and his tiny band brought new life to a large swath of Washington, DC, teetering on dramatic decline. His unique Church of the Savior birthed dozens of faith-based programs in Washington, DC, that made life infinitely better for legions of God's people in the city and beyond. I honor his grand, largely unheralded life.

The drumroll continues to include a legion of academics: The late eminent Carl Jung (1875–1961) did pioneering work with the human psyche in myriad ways, many of which are beyond my comprehension. What sticks with me of his explorations is my understanding of his thesis that our brains in the present century (make that the twenty-first) are the repository of everything in human history that has gone on before us. This is part of Jung's concept of the collective unconscious, the archetype. Do you ever feel like you've been here before, that you can almost predict what will happen in the next second? This *déjà vu* points toward Jung's belief that we have indeed been here before, not in our own bodies, but experientially, existentially. It's like an ancestor's genes from a hundred or a thousand or a dozen millennia ago suddenly telegraph a message to your brain. Your brain's receptivity synapses flash the message, "You've done this before!" So in the Jungian premise Abraham Lincoln, George Washington, Adolf Hitler, Mary Magdalene, Plato, King Tut, and even Jesus are part of me, embedded in the recesses of my wonderful brain. Maybe when Paul talked about "Christ in you, the hope of glory" (Col 1:27), he was speaking far beyond himself. That's Jung's archetype for me.

David Eagleman's book *Incognito* is a readable, thoroughly researched exploration of the wonders of the human brain. In 2013 President Barack

Obama launched an extended research program to map the human brain. Among many of Eagleman's assertions, he discusses the stupendous ways our individual brains are hardwired by the genes we have inherited from known and unknown forebears.

So what we know—and more, what we do *not* know—about our brains is staggering. I conclude from these two great thinkers the affirmation that my brain is a reservoir of the sweeping, cosmic, collective human experience. What makes me tick? I don't know much. I know so little of my own history. (I dare not begin a study of my genealogy at this point. Many of my friends have become infected with the genealogy bug, and it will not let them go. I am avoiding exposure to that bug at this point. Perhaps when I finish this book…?)

Maybe, just maybe, my bent toward life through the framework of faithing is not my own invention, certainly not mine alone. Maybe a great-great-great-aunt's genes have ratcheted up to some level of functionality in my own head. I respond to what she forwarded to me from a hundred years ago. Since I am not a robot, at a level of my existence, I choose to respond to what she sent me, making me personally responsible for what happens to me. But it's all there—or make that *here.*

For instance, most of us have seen Anderson Cooper on television doing all manner of reporting from CNN and around the world. It came as an interesting surprise to me a few years ago to learn that his mother is the famous and glamorous Gloria Vanderbilt, an heiress of the enormously wealthy nineteenth-century Vanderbilt clan of New York. Along the way Gloria met Wyatt Cooper, a writer and actor who hailed from the little town of Quitman, Mississippi, and they were married. When Anderson was ten years old, his father, only in his fifties, had a massive heart attack and died, devastating him, his brother Carter, and Gloria. In his 2016 book *The Rainbow Comes and Goes*, written with his mother, Anderson recalls the first time some years after his father's death that he returned for a family reunion in Mississippi. Cooper's reminiscences on that visit illustrate my point about the wonders and mysteries of genetic inheritances. He says,

> It was the first time I had been with [my father's] family as an adult and the thing that struck me most was seeing that I shared not just a physical resemblance with some of them, but similar gestures and

expressions. To discover that the way I laugh, or the way I brush my hand through my hair is something hard-wired in my brain, something that other Coopers had done before me and would do long after I was gone, was powerful, and made me feel connected to both the past and the future. It was a feeling I had never had before, and it has stayed with me to this day.[2]

Now, lest we think that who we are today is only a matter of psychical electricity coursing through our brains at the speed of light, a wondrous if inexplicable materialism, what about the mind? Brain, I can begin to understand. But mind, emotion, what makes me tick, what makes me an individual, where does that come from? Could it be that our brains are the great and, to this point, ultimate example of artificial intelligence? Maybe those gurus who are trying to invent computers that replicate, even match the human brain are simply trying to catch up with what evolution, God, nature, culture have already planted in us?

I have listed a few stars from my own past. As we move along, I will surely call attention to others who have contributed to my myness. As Paul says of his Philippian friends, "I count every memory of them as privilege" (Phil 1:3).

CHAPTER FOUR

Powerful Blips

Now I want to explore some of the blips of personality and attitude that seem to mark me as a man. For starters I claim an existential confidence juxtaposed with restless ambiguity.

Existential Confidence

Part of my aim in writing this memoir comes as I want to trace the dimensions of existential confidence that have long marked much of my life. That basic confidence sets the stage for an abiding peace about life and about being dead. I want to be honest as I peel that onion, but I want to peel the onion. Part of what I find beneath the peelings I will include in these pages. Part of my findings will remain my own personal pain/treasure.

Life

A trigger for this effort about life, among several, came from two identifiable sources. At a Jesus Seminar in New York City a few years ago and in some of his tapes, Lloyd Geering, a New Zealand minister and theologian, laid down an unforgettable marker for me. He said his clergy peers reached a point when they decided they could henceforth coast without serious attention to future growth. Geering, in retort, said he had reached no such plateau. He would not stop pushing, thinking, reaching out to whatever beckoned. I agree with Geering. I have so far found no place nor inclination to stop.

Another trigger got pulled when a personal friend and fellow minister queried, "What keeps you moving? Changing? Growing?"

That push, that unwillingness to stop, emerges as part and parcel of who I am as a human being. I am coming to understand that what I tag as existential confidence provides me an assurance that faithing need have no boundaries. As long as I have my mental faculties, I can never come to the end of my best mind nor transcend the Spirit of the holy, the then and the there. This confidence about life at eighty prompts me to attempt this memoir. My road twists and curves with new sign post around every bend. I am grateful for the persistent tug of that journey inward and journey outward.

Death

As to the confidence about death, I remember one night lying in my bed as a sixteen-year-old. With some classmates I had been attending high-powered Youth for Christ (YFC) rallies in Atlanta (more on that later). The revivalist always wanted us to trust Jesus Christ as Lord and Savior to make sure that when we died, we would go to heaven and not be consigned by God to an everlasting, burning hell. I thought I would go to heaven but had not fully settled that one.

Frankly, by that stage of my young life, I had all but decided hell was not for me. I began to question the existence of hell as portrayed by my preacher and the evangelist. But who was I, a mere lad, to question such a cornerstone doctrine of Baptist and YFC preaching?

Then, out of the ether that night came a breeze? a whisper? the Holy Spirit? another message from an ancestor long gone? "Bob, you need never again fear being dead." The message did not say dying would be a picnic. But being dead need hold no terror for me ever again. A part of me has lived out of that moment for these decades, giving me a strong measure of existential peace.

From time to time as the years fly by, I do come face to face with the fact of my own death. I admit some angst at the prospect of being dead. My grandson Peter and I were philosophizing one day about life and death. He said, "Bob (he calls Linda and me by our first names), someday you will be gone. I don't like to think about that." I replied to him, "Peter, I don't want to be gone from you either. But what pains me a lot about being dead is all in your life and experiences I will miss. School. Adventure. Your marriage. And all that. Besides, we've just entered a new technological era, and I hate to miss out on all that will mean in your life."

I don't want to be totally forgotten. Balancing the angst is my developing idea of passing on my best genes to Peter and future generations just as I have received the genes from ancestors. Dead, forgotten, but never fully gone.

Two sobering, face-the-music moments came to me in 2016. In the fall of 2016 a group of friends and I trekked to a Philadelphia suburb to spend the afternoon canvassing for Hillary Clinton. The weather was humid with a misting rain. After about three hours trudging up and down the hills of my solo suburban assignment, I sat down on a low rock wall to wait for Pete Davis to come and drive me to the rendezvous point and head home. I suddenly began to feel very fuzzy. I took deep breaths but had drunk all my water. The next thing I knew, a small band of passersby and EMT team were clustered around me as I lay on the ground. I had fainted dead away. Rushed to the hospital in an ambulance, I was admitted for a battery of tests and stayed overnight for observation. After a frantic call to Linda, she drove anxiously from Bethesda to Philadelphia to be told I had become seriously dehydrated in the humid afternoon. I have no memory of falling to the ground or of anyone stopping to help. I blacked out. I had no after effects but serious reflection.

Such was not the case with what happened to Linda and me on November 19, 2016. We had traveled to Panama City, Florida, where we have a family beach cottage. We had planned to spend Thanksgiving with Linda's brothers and their wives at the house. In driving through a busy intersection I did not see the oncoming car that T-boned us, smashing into my side of the car. Linda and I do not remember the actual crash nor the quick arrival of first responders. I do vaguely recall pain and despair. Ambulances rushed us to a nearby trauma hospital. The upshot is that I suffered a horribly crushed left hip. Linda was tossed around in the car, leaving her badly bruised and unable to walk for days without assistance. The net result for me was five months of rehab and therapy; two operations, laced through with anxiety, hope, and profound thankfulness for excellent medical care. Linda recovered her mobility but still undergoes physical therapy, dealing with aggravating tags from the crash. If the accident had been a bit more horrific, we both could have died. The only consolation to our children would have been that we never knew what hit us.

In both instances I came away saying to Linda and others, "This is how it is to die." One is here for a moment and gone the next. Linda and I have both spent hours reflecting on the trauma and pushing mentally and spiritually to decide what it means for us at eighty. We are grateful to our three children— Andy, Ben, and Elizabeth—and a host of family and friends who have made this long recovery journey with us more manageable. We are quietly determined to make the most of the time we have left. We both stared death in the face and lived to tell the tale.

Now more than ever, I have internalized the fact that someday, sooner or later, folks will gather at a memorial service for me and wish me well into whatever lies out there. I have decided to be cremated. I have two wishes for my remains. If I am still in the Bethesda area, I want part of my ashes interred in the lovely memorial garden at Westmoreland Congregational United Church of Christ or in the exquisite Treasure Garden at the Briggs Center's Carpenter's House. Another portion will be placed with Linda, wherever that might be. (At this point she's not sure about cremation. She has said she only wants a simple graveside service at the Cook/Holloway family plot in Thomaston, Georgia, with just the Mormon Tabernacle Choir singing the "Hallelujah Chorus." Nothing elaborate, you understand.)

Be sure I am not a "sweet by and by" person. I have had no visions of a heavenly Land of Oz. I am not a "there" person. If there is a there, that's fine with me. If there's no there, that's okay also. My persuasion is that none of us needs to fret over what's next. It would surely be silly for me to deny a there. That's completely beyond my knowing. Stories of visitations from the beyond abound. When my late friend was nine years old, her mother died. My friend went to her own grave telling the story of how her recently deceased mother appeared at the foot of her daughter's bed in the middle of the night. I don't know if the mother said anything to her bereft young daughter, but that moment of presence comforted my friend for the rest of her days. A therapist might brush aside the moment, but I do not. I have had no such visitations, nor, to the best of my understanding, do I need them. I do dream of deceased loved ones, especially of late of Mike, my funny, grand, totally undependable brother who died of neglected, untreated prostate cancer, the scourge of several male members of our family, including my father, brother, and me.

Restless Ambiguity

The other half of this personal equation is restless ambiguity. I am okay with most of life's ambiguities. I can be fairly content knowing how much I do not know. Long ago some wise person said, "If you have a simple answer to a complex question, it's probably wrong." With that advice in mind, I quickly grow impatient with folks who pontificate that they have the totally right answer. So ambiguities remain, but my restlessness pushes me to reach out to know and experience more.

Affirmations

I affirm some wonderful, freeing aspects of my journey that I pray will be helpful and liberating to others who come along after me. I will return to these affirmations along the way.

What do I affirm? I am a God person. I affirm primal energy, the primordial electricity of the universe. Pervasive. As air to the land animal, as water to the fish. As benevolent gravity. An expression of collective humanity. Greater than the sum of all our parts. Wholly other yet completely here. Maybe some measure of cosmic or immanent providence. Translate all this as God. The universe is on my side. This God is for me as love, an incomprehensible positive force. Translate that love as beckoning, demanding, evocative, embracing, and leveling. Yet I do not know any of this beyond the shadow of a doubt, nor do I need to know any of this beyond the shadow of a doubt. Existential confidence intermingles with restless ambiguity. I choose this basic affirmation as a secure place to stand. Why not? I have not come up with a better grounding. The grand old hymn says it well: "Here I raise my Ebenezer. Hither by thy help I've come" (1 Sam 7:12; from "Come Thou Fount of Every Blessing").

I emphatically affirm I am a Jesus person, existentially, first, last, and always. In the next breath I readily, even gratefully announce that this declaration is full of delightful, important ambiguities. The ambiguities, rather than putting me down, energize my faithing journey. This ever-present Jesus remains an axial figure in world history and increasingly in my own journey.

As far back as I can remember, Jesus has been part of my consciousness. My most vivid early experience with Jesus came after a hair-raising revival in our Baptist church when I was about 13. The preacher had laid out his terrifying and fabricated description of the second coming of Jesus—thundering horses, fire, yawning hell, avenging angels all in store for those who had not accepted Jesus as savior from sin in their lives. He said nothing about the love of God or the care of a loving savior. For weeks afterward I would wake up in the night seeing a nighttime glow outside my window. "Jesus," I would cry out silently, "if this is you coming back, please come into my trembling heart. Save me so I won't go to hell." Not a happy time with Jesus, for sure. Fortunately, time and a much clearer understanding of the book of Revelation enabled me to encounter a different, already-on-my-side Jesus.

So at eighty: affirmation and ambiguity. I will never know definitively if Jesus' grave was really empty that dawn when Mary showed up with her spices. I am a Jesus person regardless of what was going on with his body after he died on the cross. I am quick to say that I am indebted to my ancient cousins writing some thirty or forty years after the crucifixion who reported the grave empty. They pass on to me via a 2,000-year-old cumulative tradition the throbbing story of an ever-living Jesus who continues to shape my life, and the life of the world, to this day.

Thus, my experience of the living Jesus becomes all the more emphatic thanks to this towering concept of cumulative tradition given to us by the late Harvard professor W. Cantwell Smith in his prescient book *The Meaning and End of Religion*. More, much more, on Smith's idea of cumulative tradition as we move along. I will also most assuredly spend more time talking about Jesus, blending together a comfortable mix of history, cumulative Christian tradition archetype, and genetics.

I affirm prayer, though I know very little of the mechanics, if there be such, of the effort of praying. After fairly extensive reading about the psyche of us humans across the ages and in just about every clime, I come away saying we humans are a praying species. Regardless of one's theology, we all pray in good times and bad by reflex, like breathing. When even the most resolutely non-religious father gets news his son is near death from a terrible car crash, he prays. To whom and for what vary infinitely. But we pray. My best explanation for the effectiveness of prayer is that my praying for you—be you next door or around the globe—creates an energy field that through the wonders and mysteries of physics gets transmitted to you. Consciously or unconsciously, you receive the energy—the love energy, one sage has posited—that I send in your direction. So I pray for my ailing grandson; for the very human, often stumbling political leaders; for the victims of that roaring tornado that bore down on an Illinois village, leveling everything in its screaming path; for the victims and their families of our nation's nearly total collective indifference to gun violence; for immigrant fleeing violence.

I affirm a providence, a moving, calling, shaping force, that has animated me for decades. I revel in this sense of purpose while readily admitting I know little about this force. I make this affirmation more from anecdotal experience than from any neat theological or teleological formulation.

With the same measure of exuberance, I make it known that I am a Christian Bible person. Writing this memoir reminds me that the Bible has been the most pervasively present book in my life from about age twelve. Southern Baptist churches of that era of the 1950s sponsored competition "Sword Drills" as a way for kids to learn their way around in the Bible. The Bible for us was the "sword of the LORD" (see Ezek 20). In a quasi-military way we kids competed with each other to find and recite verses, books, and characters in the Bible as our leader gave commands: "Attention! Draw swords! Charge!" I did not learn much of what the Bible said or meant, but I could find Ruth or Colossians or Psalm 8 in blinding speed. That Bible was fun and challenging. Today, it pains me to see fellow church members on Sunday morning fumble to find the sermon text in the pew Bible. Thankfully, years later, not only could I quickly find Philippians 2; I could get inside the glorious poetry Paul used to embrace the cosmic Jesus.

One of my favorite people, a lifelong Quaker/agnostic, had a way of saying, "What's with this Bible routine? Every time you preach, you use the Bible!" I would reply, "Frank, the Bible is my book as a Christian preacher." At the same time, my long, invigorating encounter with the Christian Bible raises many ambiguities. I will talk about these as we move along, but I am okay with what I know, what I think I know, and what I do not know about the Bible, my book, as a Christian person. Why the Bible? Why not? The Bible gathers up the collective yearning of multiplied millions of fellow pilgrims to connect with that other and that here. The Bible can be painfully distorted, but so can CNN. The Bible can bless (and curse) at whatever level one encounters it. The Bible can be peeled like the onion, but at its core it's green like life.

I am a church person. I need a faith community, a human garden, in which I can grow, find comfort in times of stress, laced through with the freedom, even the encouragement, to push to the outer limits of my own spiritual universe. The church, with all its warts, is the signal institution that aims to embrace every human person, child, youth, adult, single, married, divorced, gay, straight, transgender, honorable, and, like all of us, quite flawed.

I express the deepest gratitude for the congregations that let me partner with them as pastor: First Baptist Church, Vienna, Georgia; First Baptist Church, Calhoun, Georgia; Mayfield Road Baptist Church, Arlington, Texas; and especially the Briggs Baptist Church, Bethesda, Maryland. Briggs Church, which I had the honor to lead from 1992 until 2006, provided the freedom for me to push around in and through an exciting if sometimes rather sophomoric era of personal, theological, and academic reset. My active church ministry concluded with six exhilarating years (2006–2012) at the Westmoreland Congregational United Church of Christ, Bethesda, Maryland, where I was first a member of the staff. Then for two years I served as interim senior pastor with two grand colleagues while the church sought and ultimately called a dear friend and wonderfully able minister, Rev. Timothy B. Tutt. More later on this part of my journey.

As you are concluding, my faithing journey has taken me through many theological, vocational, political, spiritual, and personal iterations, yet I have experienced a basic grounding of existential confidence within many zigs and zags.

My bias? When I look in the well that is the Christians tradition and Bible, especially the New Testament, the reflection I see may be none other than my own. For many years I had hunches that what I had been taught in Sunday school, college, and seminary about Jesus, the Gospels, Paul, and the evolution of the Jesus movement were superficial, tips of the iceberg. Even in those early days I felt short-changed. I did not know what I did not know; I just knew there was more to know. Many questions persisted, and vague hunches plagued me, but I had little time and few tools to help me existentially and theologically deal with my short-changed hunch. I realize now that many of my Baptist university and seminary professors (1955–1963), who probably knew more than they said, lived with and worked within cultural and bureaucratic restraints. Baptist religious life in the Deep South in those post-World War II years of the last century did not invite or permit much serious thinking and talking outside the cultural box. If the professors knew better, for fear of their jobs, for the most part, they did not say better. Sad to say, the situation is not much improved among most Southern Baptist preachers and teachers of their ilk these days, where propaganda goes under the guise of education. I celebrate that theological liberation found new force and content during my halcyon days in doctoral work at Candler School of Theology, Emory University, in Atlanta. Still, soon after completing the degree in 1975, exciting changes entered my life that essentially took me out of the theological loop for nearly fifteen years.

I reentered the theological loop in 1992 when, thankfully, I had my own renaissance as I became the pastor of Briggs Church. Now, during the past twenty-five years I have embraced, for me, new wisdom. Flowing from the heart and pens of many scholars, this newness calls into serious question most everything I had assumed and/or been taught about historic Christianity. The new prompts me completely to rethink traditional theology and biblical studies, especially involving the New Testament.

Almost breathlessly, I hasten to say that rather than jettisoning all the initial orthodoxy, I have built on that tradition to come to a perspective that makes sense to me in the light of my own decades of living, serious study, and consistent searching. In these years I have moved away from often unsettling confusion to a place of existential peace juxtaposed with restless ambiguity.

Standing on the shoulders of a host of courageous women and men who dared respond to their own search for honesty, I am in the process of claiming my own faithing at eighty, embracing a journey into energizing and liberating theological, biblical, and existential poetry and imagination.

As you may have noticed by now, in this effort I will not labor much with footnotes. I will give attribution where I can; you are welcome to call me out when you run across an idea or thread you can trace to this or that author. I say honestly and shamelessly that countless friends, authors, books, conferences, stories, tapes, DVDs, Discovery Channel documentaries, and conversations are all here. At the end of the book, I will list some of the authors and their works I know have meant the world to me and whom I commend to the reader. I offer deepest thanks to everyone in that great cloud of witnesses who yet hover around me.

What do I want to accomplish with this effort? Rather than autobiography in a traditional sense, it is a personally important selective skip down my memory lane. I hope to convey the fulfilling sense of personal spiritual security I experience despite the vicissitudes of daily life. I point toward an all-embracing, no-holds-barred adventure, especially at the existential level of the worldview that animates me.

Hear me carefully when I say mine is a not a willy-nilly relativism. My faithing is rooted in the overall biblical message, taken seriously if not always literally. To the best of my mind and ability, flowing through the grand river of cumulative tradition, my faithing is existentially connected to Jesus of

Nazareth through 2,000 years of twisting but often productive history. With Jesus as mentor, I am profoundly persuaded, using Pierre Teilhard de Chardin's seminal concept of Christ as cosmic Omega point, that we mortals are on a journey of Star Trek proportions as we zoom through hitherto unexplored, innermost dimensions of the human spirit. I hope you will find yourself here in real ways. As we walk together, I hope you can locate even greater security, freedom, and grace in your own faithing journey of whatever stripe and flavor it might be—faithing toward freedom.

CHAPTER FIVE
Sailing on the Sea of Faith

Paul Tillich once said, "Faith is the capacity to say yes to life and death." In her book *The Preaching Life*, Barbara Brown Taylor writes, "When all's said and done, faith may be nothing more than the assignment of holy meaning to events that others call random."[3] Cantwell Smith says something like, "Faith is personal faith. This is an inner religious experience of a particular person. Faith is the personal experience of the transcendent, imagined or real."[4] Christian Wiman in *My Bright Abyss* poetically affirms, "Faith is not some hard, unchanging thing you cling to through the vicissitudes of life. Those who try to make it into this are destined to become brittle, shatterable creatures.... Faith (as a human experience) is within the natural order.... When all is said and done, faith is folded into change, is the mutable, and messy process of our lives rather than any fixed, mental process."[5] I opt for a faithing perspective along these lines—hope and confidence tethered to the admittedly cosmic immutable.

An amorphous but pervasive otherness frames my life as the years roll by. My personal faithing points me toward the transcendent, though I am comfortable with little or no definition of that transcendent. Not in a long time, maybe never, have I felt a need to define, box in, predetermine my perspective on faithing. Faithing is broad and pervasive. Faithing is not a rabbit's foot or a magical, mystical Ouija board. Wishing hard, praying hard, sitting on a hillside contemplating, or collecting a crowd of fellow beseechers for a long time about something I want to happen gives me no assurance it will happen. If I direct my faithing toward God, I need fully to understand that God has no responsibility to do what I want, no matter how much faithing I might be able to conjure up. At that same time, a faithing perspective is real for me. I have an existential confidence in my faithing perspective that sustains in the midst of layers of ambiguities that nurture a healthy restlessness.

Many ways occur to me to get at this faithing thing. I offer some serendipitous metaphors.

Faithing *That*, Not Faithing *In*

When I think about my faithing perspective, I can put it this way: With Cantwell Smith I have faith (God-tethered confidence) *that* more than faith (confidence) *in*.[6] This becomes a good starting point of faith*ing* for me. Faithing means, for me, that life and even the universe finally make sense. Faithing undergirds my sense of hope in the ultimate rationality of creation, of the human race, in the working out of a plan or a system or a providence that is completely beyond my ability to spell it out or predict any outcomes. Faithing assures me that indeed all things do work together for good, as Paul declares (Rom 8:28), even when I cannot begin to sort it all through and even when the world seems to be going to hell in a handbasket.

The long history of life on the planet underscores my faithing *that*. The forming of the primordial dust into our own existence points me to toward faithing *that*. From the time we could walk upright, we have inflicted pain and suffering on one another. We have come close to destroying rivers, fields, and the air. Still, in all, wrongs gradually get righted. Dictators fall. We sin, individually and nationally, and then manage to move on.

Faithing *in* suggests, I surmise, that maybe I can count, erroneously, on a more precise arrangement to life. Even to say "faith *in* God" does not work very well for me. An assertion of faith in God pushes me to try to define God. Faith in God can nudge me to locate God in a given religious outlook. I do not want to fall into the human trap that prompts me to put God in any sort of box. At any rate my personal understanding of God is too broad to fit within any known religious, political, or social system.

What's more, I have faith *that* rather than *in* the way of Jesus. This linguistic snatch persuades me that the Jesus way leads to all manner of positive results in my life and in the world. Some writers translate the phrase "faith in Jesus" to mean "the faith of Jesus." The faith of Jesus provides a helpful theological shift for me. Rather than conjuring up the notion of faith in Jesus leading to fullness of life and heaven, I can readily appreciate that when I can appropriate the quality of faith that motivated Jesus, I can be on the road to a significantly more robust life today with no real concern for what lies out there beyond this existence. Faith in Jesus puts Jesus on a theological pedestal he never sought for himself. To go for a Godward faith like Jesus makes Jesus and me partners, colleagues in the work of God's ways in the world.

Experiential Faith

My faithing is experiential far more than doctrinal or formulaic. At the risk of sounding overly grand, mine is a restless faith that throbs with life. My faithing perspective shapes, limits, expands, energizes my full life.

My faithing generates a confidence that there is always more than meets the eye. Recently, I ran across an article about a new digital camera trained on the heavens. The writer said the camera would be able to make pictures of thousands and thousands of galaxies, not just plain old ordinary stupendous stars. Myriads of galaxies. Zillions of light years away. The article made me catch my breath for a minute. Galaxies? Maybe King David had the same thought when he asked of God, "What is man that you are mindful of him?" (Ps 8).

Who are we? What are we? Where did all this wondrous creation come from? More, much more, than meets the eye—even the eye of that new digital camera—is out there and in here. Talking about death one day with Peter, my wonderfully wise young grandson, I told him, "My biggest pain at the thought of dying smacks me when I think of all that I will miss in your life, Peter, by dying." Being dead—what a waste, how pedestrian and ordinary! I embrace mystery, otherness, beyondness, but not out *there* in a religious sense. The beyondness frames me not in the sweet by and by, but now, in the midst of living. Faithing as the possibility of thereness and assurance of hereness undergirds my life at eighty.

Faith as Possibilitarianism

David Eagleman, whom I mentioned earlier, and others of his ilk are hacking out an approach to life and beyond, popularly called possibilitarianism. Eagleman's comprehensive study of the human brain, specifically, and existence in several places prompts him to suggest atheism is too arrogant while agnosticism is too wishy-washy for him. He opines that given the richness of human life, the dynamism of the engine of life, the brain, the transcendental extension of the brain into the human mind, genes, the staggering quantum scope and connectedness of all creation, the tiny organisms and the massive dimensions of the universe persuade him that anything is possible. All these possibilities are not apparent. Indeed, only a few emerge at this point. They are not demonstrable but possible, maybe even real, beyond our capacity to know or imagine at this point. Some unremembered observer has offered the extraordinary concept of "universal soul," a soul, an innerness, that embraces all of the created order. We exist as part of the eternal atomic structure of that soul. Maybe this is Albert Einstein's elusive search for the universal principle that connects all of creation.

Something like possibilitarianism can work for me at this point. Okay, you might say, I can just stop reading here. If this possibilitarianism means that everything's going to pan out all right in the end, why fret now? I can go on my merry way, doing the best I can.

You could adopt that *laissez-faire* attitude, but it does not suit me. Nor has it satisfied countless other explorers of the human spirit, of the created world, or of the universe.

Let me play out possibilitarianism a bit. For me this notion cobbles together the infinite reaches of the human brain with finite capacities of the human spirit with the incredible dimensions of genetics. Toss in the developing notion of epigenetics, human possibilities that go beyond the chemistry of genetics. Then stir in Carl Jung's generative theory of collective unconsciousness. Next take even a cursory look at overall, albeit ragged and tragic, human progress over the past several millennia. Into all this mix, blend in what has happened before our individual and collective eyes for the past century, and I come away with possibilitarianism. Add to this potpourri my amorphous sense of faithing, and I can be more sanguine about the future, despite the politics, inanities, irritations, and terrorisms of everyday life.

Of course, any oft-tried recipes, metaphysical or physical, can fail. Melba's classic pound cake can flop, particularly with guests on the way to the house for dessert, regardless of how many times the recipe has worked like a charm. Frankly, when the cake crashes, I have to admit that it's the fault of the chef rather than the recipe. Melba's recipe succeeds far more times than it misses.

Possibilitarianism. Maybe I can sleep better at night with a quiet confidence that someone, something, some force, some energy has "hands" on the switch. At the same time we all know that crazy, zany, totally inexplicable, haphazardly explainable explosions and implosions happen all the time. Does the one in charge of the universe's switch doze off every now and then? I don't know, but the way I do faithing helps me maneuver through those times when all hell breaks loose, when the center does not seem to hold.

At the same time my existential confidence in my own ability to manage keeps me at the switch of my own life. Do I doze off every now and then? Yes. Does stuff in my own life go haywire? Did you not see that red car barreling down on you at the intersection? You have that one right.

I was sitting at my desk at Westmoreland Church the afternoon the 2010 earthquake rumbled through greater Washington, DC. I had never experienced an earthquake, yet in the few seconds of the rattle and roll, I knew that the ground beneath our collective feet had just convulsed. I had no control whatso-ever over that mighty shake. The Washington Monument on the National Mall shook, requiring millions of dollars for extensive repairs. The majestic Washington National Cathedral, almost within my sight line, sustained millions of dollars in damage to the twin towers that inspire one and all as we gaze upward at their majesty. Hereafter, all new big construction projects in our region will have to take into account the hitherto unnoticed reality of earthquakes. We cannot control earthquakes, but we would be silly to ignore the ramifications in real time if and when we experience another powerful tremor.

My faithing kicks in at these quirky junctures. I now know that the unheard of—make that all manner of earthquakes—can happen in my backyard. If I come away from those quakes in one piece, physically alive and breathing, my faithing praxis persuades me I can manage though battered and bruised, forever marked.

In this calculus of faithing experience, I embrace a measure of cognition, of reason. My background—dealing with life, my own and others; reading history; just watching television news—persuades me that such serendipities can be managed. But the head trip is not enough. I claim something from within and beyond, from my own physicality, and energy from genes gifted by known and unknown ancestors that will enable me and mine to rise to fight another day. If I do not physically survive the earthquake, I rely on faithing that persuades me my own genes will transmit to those whom I now know as family. And what's more, my own genes will join that great, real, if ephemeral human river of life that flows inexorably forward. Thirty or forty years from now, grandchildren Will, Jake, Luke, Peter, or Georgia will face an earthquake of their own and find within themselves, from Linda or me, without realizing the source, the wherewithal to rebuild that which fell apart.

Sailing on the Sea of Faith

Don Cupitt of England, one of my favorite and certainly most theologically radical thinkers, describes his own approach to life and, yes, faith as "sailing on the sea of faith." At a point in his life, Cupitt produced and presented a six-series program on BBC he called "The Sea of Faith." Cupitt relished the idea of sailing on the sea of faith, going where the tides of the very real but tumultuous sea took him spiritually and theologically. He came in for a barrage of criticism from many theological academics in England at the time, but the series reportedly struck a powerful chord with thousands in the British public. They, with Cupitt, savor the notion of sailing on the sea of faith. As Cupitt and many of his fellow Brits moved beyond traditional Christian orthodoxy, the idea of cutting loose and sailing with the tides apparently held great appeal and logic.

So as a key metaphor for faithing at eighty, I relish the notion of sailing on the sea of faith, going where the very real (nothing unreal about the seas) but serendipitous tides take me. Legitimate questions arise. Am I just drifting with no sail or rudder or compass? Am I on the sea of faith alone? Who built the "vessel" in which I sail? And who taught me to sail in the first place?

Look at it this way: The life of faithing at eighty, sailing on the sea of faith at eighty, encompasses emotional queasiness, unknown destination/ETA, regnant promises of high adventure, and a heady declaration that I am navigating my own ship while assisted by a grand and able, if unseen, crew (the cumulative Christian tradition). What more could a guy with eight decades at his back ask?

Queasiness

When I started my own journey on the sea of faith these decades ago and began to encounter hitherto unanticipated winds and tides, I became queasy, nervous. What if my hunches lead me down a long and lonely road at the end of which lay only everlasting damnation? That's scary to a young man then canoeing in a relatively calm, traditional Southern Baptist pond.

Destination

When I started (What *is* "started"?), certainly my destination was unknown. If I thought about destination, with little notion that I puzzled much on that subject, I had no idea where I was headed. The further along I sailed on this sea, the more familiar shores receded from sight. From time to time, I did cast a wondering, even nervous eye on the disappearing shore, but like Jonathan

Livingston Seagull (Richard Bach, 1970) the relative comfort of the familiar shore held insufficient charm to prevent me from pushing on.

ETA

The longer I have sailed, the greater the thrill. My main concern has come with the desire just to stay afloat, to keep sailing, tacking with the wind and tides. The estimated time of arrival matters not at all. In fact, I had and have no notion of arriving anywhere in this life. And to the best of my knowledge, I have no concern about the final destination beyond what we have come to call this life, this expression of human existence. Do I still get nervous on this sea of faith? Yes, but the jitters only last for a brief time.

My Crew

Most of all—and here the metaphors really get mixed—I am not sailing alone. Linda and our family are with me in both a real and mystical sense. I look around in my small boat and feel, if not see, the abiding help of a great host of folks who have likewise sailed their tiny vessels on the breast of their own sea of faith. When the winds howl or when becalmed, with no shore in sight, when I have run out my own meager string as a sailor, I take existential confidence that a great host of folks have likewise ventured out from their own known shores. The genes of long-forgotten or never-known ancient mariners yet course through the cosmos of my own existence to say, "Sail on! We make the voyage with you." Some of these you might know. Jesus of Nazareth certainly sailed his own version of the sea of faith. Paul the missionary to the Roman Empire, women and men barely mentioned on the pages of history, and some like Martin Luther and Martin Luther King Jr. and Jimmy Carter and Robert Funk and Marcus Borg and Dominic Crossan, Elaine Pagels, Bill Rogers, Tony Martin, Tim Tutt, and Linda Maddox have likewise embarked in an oft-lonely but ultimately transformative voyage on the sea of faith.

So, you see, though in the boat by myself, I am not alone at all. In ways you may not see, if you have read even this far, you are in the boat with me as I am in the boat with you.

High Adventure

If you don't get anything else from this literary effort, feel the sense of high adventure that has permeated the journey. On Easter Sunday morning 1980, my family and I led the sunrise service at Camp David for President and Mrs. Carter and a small crowd of their family and White House friends. After breakfast some of us dads hid Easter eggs for the small children. I looked across the sloping lawn and saw the president leaning over bushes tucking eggs out of sight. It came to me then and stays: a Baptist preacher from Georgia hiding Easter eggs at Camp David with the president of the United States. It doesn't get any better than this. High adventure.

Risk Taking the Wheel of My Own Vessel

Risk? Yes. Not alone, but it's my ship, my life, my faithing. I'll take the chances.

Faithing as Generative Energy

Another faithing blip on the sea of faith that has stayed with me for a long time comes to me as the generative power of emphatic faithing. Energetic, robust, tested, examined, even if amorphous, faithing has within its embrace significant power. That measure of existential confidence can go in all manner of creative directions. My father, as far as I know, had never sold anything in his first forty years of life. He worked with his hands, a maintenance man in a large Atlanta office building during the Depression when he and Mother married in 1931. Upon moving to Norfolk Navy Yard at the beginning of World War II, he set about to do electrical work on massive troop transport ships. After the war he learned the burgeoning air conditioning trade. When he and Mother resettled us in Atlanta, he picked up again as an electrician. In 1950 he and Mother made the tumultuous decision that he would make a huge leap and become a professional salesman. He would sell commercial janitorial supplies to huge cotton mills, now long gone, businesses and schools in Southwest Georgia.

"Can you do this?" someone might have asked. Can you make this abrupt change in your life? If he had doubts, I never heard them from him. He had that measure of faith-generated confidence in himself and by then a growing connection to God (thanks to the Billy Graham revivals he attended). His robust if uncritical faithing provided a generous source of generative power. He became a charismatic and successful salesman of, as he said, "soap."

This story of generative faithing is repeated infinitely in large and small ways.

Jack Carter told me one day in 1975, "My father is going to run for president."

"President of what?" many of us asked.

"President of the United States!"

Jimmy Carter of Plains, Georgia, had the measure of faith in himself, in his heritage, with God that enabled him to become president of the United States of America. Beyond the four years in office, he has become one of the greatest men of our time: humanitarian, healer of nations, Nobel Peace Prize recipient, author of nearly thirty books, Sunday school teacher par excellence, husband, father, grandfather, and world statesman.

Faithing Perspective: Cumulative Christian Tradition

My faithing perspective is basically religious, my own reach for and into the transcendent, if you let me lay out religion as I understand it. Religion at its bare-boned roots means to choose. We human beings have long chosen worldviews that seek to relate to the beyondness, the otherness, the unseen but real elements of human existence. Religion, then, evolves as a human invention. From time immemorial we humans have chosen a wide variety of approaches to deal with what we do not know. Faced with life's unremitting complexities, we humans have crafted approaches to deal with everyday existence. Religion, then, comes from, grows from that choice or set of choices. Faithing along selected paths expresses our human confidence that what we have chosen as a fundamental perspective is true, dependable, meaningful for ourselves.

Human culture shapes religion. Our praxis begins at least as a product of the community in which we are born and nurtured—Christian, Hindu, Muslim, Jewish, etc. For these reasons we can never honestly say that ours is the only way to God, that Other, whatever we seek to know and/or fear.

My faithing is shaped by the ever-unfolding Christian tradition. I have come to revel in and recoil from aspects of that Christian tradition we humans have transmitted across the past two millennia. Think about some of the awful apocalypses we have inflicted on the world in the name of that one religious tradition. To stay afloat on the Christian sea of faith, for years I ducked my head and pushed on regardless of the traumas we have caused. I stayed at it because we have also wrought magnificent, positive, upwardly mobile changes in the world. A few years ago, I found another of those significant tools of thought that have made my life better. I earlier mentioned Cantwell Smith's prescient idea of "cumulative tradition." Now, with my head a bit clearer at this stage of my life, I can say I am a product of the cumulative Christian tradition that has been handed down to me.

The personal faithing that finds roots in and grows out of that cumulative Christian tradition is appreciative of but not bound by widely accepted Christian stories that have become dogma. I do not have to rest my faithing perspective on literal acceptance of these classics. At the same time I am grateful for the stories. Many of my Christian forbears firmly believed in these narratives as hard facts. Their beliefs in these stories gave strong underpinnings to their ability to establish, shape, and pass on their grasp of the Jesus movement to me and mine. But for my part in the twenty-first century, I do not have to give mental assent to these narratives to firmly root myself in the Christian tradition. From those narratives, from the energy of those who held unquestioningly to them, the religion called "Christianity" emerged. Ironically, the stories that shaped the religion need not be necessarily facts of history to have played a vital role in creating the religious tradition that I cherish in my own time.

The perspective I regard as religious that shapes my worldview gives me vital frames of reference for living and for viewing the world. At the same time this generous praxis so essential to my life in the twenty-first century liberates me. I do not have to force my mind and understanding of science and history into a tight box small enough and tightly built enough to accommodate dogmas generated from stories crafted 2,000 years ago.

Today, one could even provide me with incontrovertible historical proof that Jesus of Nazareth never lived, and I could still root myself in the cumulative Christian tradition that I have received. Are facts not important? Yes, they are, but deeply held beliefs are not often changed by presentation of facts, especially if one is existentially wedded to beliefs dearer than life itself. We attach ourselves to politicians and ideologies that have little or no regard for facts, yet we far too often cling to these people and their ideas tenaciously. One candidate recently declared he could shoot someone on the street and still not lose many of those who support him. Sad but probably true. For reasons that totally blow me away, my ancestors in the antebellum South were absolutely convinced that slavery was a good thing, a fact of human existence ordained by God. They vigorously insisted that the white people of the South were uniquely positioned by God to manage and hold slaves, who were blessed because of their servitude. Go figure! I never heard of a southern white person offering to trade places with one of those wonderfully blessed enslaved people. Some recent studies reveal that those old slavery notions do not die easily. One study has suggested that racism in the South remains strongest in areas of the plantation culture that held the most slaves.

Faithing Without Boundaries

My faithing is without boundaries. I sail on the sea of faith with the tides and winds. Wherever those tides and winds take, I go eagerly if sometime cautiously. At the same time, as I have previously noted, my perspective is not relativistic, rootless. Others have sailed the sea of faith and left records of their journey; accounts that shape and embolden my approaches are informed by history, the Bible, the long scope of the Christian tradition, and my twenty-first-century understanding of Jesus. For sure I now have a different take on much that was given me as fact. As Marcus Borg often said in books, lectures, and recordings, "The events may not have happened exactly as they have come down to us, but they are true anyway." How ridiculous, how totally unnecessary to toss away the classic stories because they do not fit my twenty-first-century worldview of science or history. At the same time how unproductive, even counterproductive, to try to take them literally and, more to the point, have my faithing impugned if I take a different slant on the classic stories. Again, the mantra fits for me: Take the Bible seriously but not necessarily literally.

I reserve the existential room to pick and choose what I do and do not take historically. I take the existence of the ancient Hebrews literally. I take their long struggle to know Yahweh and walk in "his" ways historically. Paul, Peter, and Jesus had real birthdays. I ascribe to the historical development of the Galilean movement that began with Jesus and after him with his brother James as the movement shifted to Jerusalem. Paul walked the roads of the Roman Empire as the Jesus story missionary to all who would listen. These are facts of history even if the contours of the development remain quite murky.

The fun and liberating part for me comes when I do not have to dot every traditional "i" to remain animated by the Christian tradition. Fortunately, I live and serve in a social and theological climate that not only accepts my evolving notions but encourages me in my pursuits, pursuits that have no discernible boundaries. I ache for fellow pilgrims, especially clergy in southern churches. Some at least want to push ahead but are bound by local culture and money that curtail or choke off serious faith discoveries.

Again remember, I am a Jesus person. Twenty-five years ago, I could not make that affirmation with such vim and vigor. Looking back on my years, until my watershed Marcus Borg event in 1992, I had mixed feelings about Jesus. I was vaguely uneasy with traditional dogma: Jesus, one man, dying for the sins of the entire world for all of human history? That's a lot to swallow. Why did he "have" to die? Why could God not figure another way to save the world from sin other than kill Jesus?

For the first thirty or so of my years as a minister, I could be comfortable preaching about God. I confidently preached that the way of Jesus held much good and promise for all of us. I found great adventure in living within the Christian ethos. I wanted folks to connect with the church, to experience baptism, to gather for communion. But I simply could not get all worked up about Jesus as the Christ, as the one and only unique and eternal Son of God. Early on, I could not buy the assertion that only a rational, rather rote belief in Jesus assured one of heaven in the next life.

Then, in 1992, reading Marcus Borg's book *Meeting Jesus Again for the First Time*, I found the Jesus I had been looking for over the previous thirty-five or forty years. (As this memoir unfolded, I was grieved to learn of Marcus Borg's death in 2015 after a lengthy illness.) Borg's writings, lectures, and my cherished if brief personal relationship with him had a powerful impact on me and propelled this present effort. Marcus Borg, John Dominic Crossan, John Shelby Spong, John A. T. Robertson, Elaine Pagels (2016 recipient of the presidential National Humanities Medal), the Jesus Seminar, and more make earnest and reverent attempts to pull back the layers the post-Easter Jesus movement imposed on the pre-Easter Jesus of Nazareth. Encounters with these committed Christian scholars brought new life to me. Their combined labors revealed for me the grand, unique, gifted, charismatic, very human man full of God who walked and talked in the hills of Galilee. His powerful message of the kingdom of God and unbrokered relationship with God earned him the fury of the Jewish religio-political establishment. This grand human being ultimately died on a cross at the hands of the Roman Empire. The imperial regime would not brook any person, even a Galilean peasant, who dared question the power and authority of the sitting emperor, even if most of the sitting emperors did not sit very long. Assassins regularly dispatched one for another man foolish enough to think he would be the one to control the sprawling empire.

That Jesus I could know. That Jesus I could relate to. That Jesus I could attempt to emulate. That Jesus made sense to me. For me it was a time of profound personal and theological renaissance. In a sense, in that Jesus "my faith found a resting place," echoing words of the old hymn. Not in a stagnant sense, not in a passive way, I could breathe easily around this Jesus. In my own way I could take up his cross, metaphorically to be sure, and follow him into the struggle for justice, human dignity, and sexual and racial inclusiveness.

And here another important part of my Jesus story kicks in: I claim an existential, experiential, spiritual relationship with this Jesus. He and I connect. I get him. What a relief. What do I mean by "an existential, experiential, spiritual relationship"? It means that I can have a visceral connection with Jesus of Nazareth. Borg talks about secondhand and firsthand faith relationships. Secondhand faith is handed down, filtered through ecclesiastical authority in a conventional cloak that becomes normative for the Christian life. This secondhand, boxed-in faith tends to be doctrinal, formulaic, moralistic, and eschatological. "This *is* the way! The Bible says it; I believe it; that settles it!"[7]

Going for a firsthand faith puts one more nearly in a personal relationship with Jesus. I have sought a firsthand relationship with Jesus, all the while recognizing that I live in a Jewish/Christian tradition handed to me by forbears from across thousands of years. Borg emphasizes that embracing firsthand Jesus faith experience opens one to a more transformational faith centered in the Spirit that animated Jesus. This is my aim, though anything but accomplished.

Let's go in this direction: Jesus is not my savior in the traditional theological sense because in a traditional, theological, eschatological way, I am not lost. I certainly make no high-ground, moralistic declarations about myself. I face huge growing and developing challenges for sure. But not lost and bound for Dante's hell. Rather than savior from eternal punishment, in a real way Jesus becomes part of me, and I become part of him. My existential, experiential relationship with Jesus sets me more nearly on that unfolding, beckoning, transformational faithing journey.

Remember, Carl Jung talked about the collective unconscious. He talked about archetypes. He and thinkers following in his train suggest that my human brain becomes a depository of everything that has gone on before me. Jung probably didn't know about DNA. He did understand existential connections stretching the length of human existence. What I glean from Jung points me to the assertion that in a way that I cannot know quantitatively but can affirm existentially, Jesus is part of me. I appropriate the classic Pauline notion "Christ in you" genetically, archetypically, as part of the vast 2,000-year-old collective unconscious; Jesus is part of me, and I am part of Jesus in a firsthand experiential relationship for which I am deeply grateful. I also have to say again that a bunch of bad people from antiquity are also part of me. The challenge for me in my time is to let the Jesus part become ascendant, take precedence, dominate all the bad stuff that likewise lurks in my incredible brain.

With Jesus in me and me in Jesus, I can more intentionally set about my own calling to do the work and ministry of Jesus in my time. I really can make a difference in my corner of the world. Of course, I am not the savior of the world, but neither was Jesus. He never claimed anything like that for himself. The post-Easter developing Jesus movement that became the church made those reverential, stupendous, imperial claims about him, but not Jesus himself.

I quickly say, however, the way of Jesus can effect great saving benefits to all of humanity for all of time. To use Dom Crossan's phrase, Jesus' unbrokered, compassionate call for life as citizens of the kingdom of God, the place of God, in our own time can make a monumental difference in the way we treat one another. The way Jesus reached beyond himself can expand an active practice of love one to another. He blessed children, included women, respected non-Jews, all expressions of his generous humanness, practices largely countercultural in his time. He faced down the local royal governor, fed the hungry, and effected healing among many of his sick, culturally unclean, and deranged neighbors with no strings attached. Whereas he cherished his Jewish heritage at its best, he did his work without calling on or relying upon the established religious leaders. He demonstrated a lack of concern for the stifling ways of the Jerusalem temple system. The Gospel writers have him paying little notice of the prevailing cultural purity laws that dominated his Jewish world. In a host of these and other ways, he showed ordinary people they could enter into the quality of firsthand relationship with God without the trappings of accepted religious routines that subverted honest contact with the Holy. Such flagrant disregard was not lost on the powerful ecclesiastical establishment that had cast lots with the Roman occupiers. Jesus' approach to life and praxis, though fraught with danger, nonetheless infuses powerful saving grace to any of us any day of the week. So I have existential confidence that Jesus can continue to make powerful if unsettling differences in the world. My affirmation that Jesus was possessed with a spirit grand and unique mitigates, if not sets aside, a need for me to have trust in Jesus as some type of universal eschatological savior.

Who was God to Jesus? Jesus probably had a simple if magisterial immanent concept of God. Encouraging to me in my journey, I perceive Jesus was never satisfied with his walk with God. He was constantly trying to get a clearer fix on God for himself and his friends. We can forget that ancient Jews had long found the freedom of spirit and relationship to question the works of God, the justice of God, the purposes of God. Read the psalms to experience the way our Jewish ancestors quarreled with God while never questioning the reality of the Holy One. The Gospel writers remember Jesus pleading with God in Gethsemane: "Let this cup pass from me" (Matt. 26:39). And from the cross: "My God, why have you forsaken me?" (Matt 27:46). At the same time "Do you believe in God?" would not have entered the mind of Jesus nor any other faithful Jew.

Jesus was well versed in Hebrew scriptures with God as the central figure. God worked directly in the affairs of humans and also worked through individuals and through the larger sweep of history. The ancient Jews, using the linguistic and philosophical tools at their disposal, generally had an anthropomorphic understanding of God. They understood God as masculine, though some smaller, more poetic writings in Scripture make room for a feminine side of God, Sophia, wisdom. One prayed to God, and God responded as he/she chose. Over the thousand years it took to write and edit the Hebrew scriptures, the texts move from a notion of God as a warlord calling the shots for people like Abraham, Moses, and Joshua to that of the God of justice, concerned not only for the Jews but for all people. Did Jesus understand himself as a son of God in a way begotten, singly, uniquely by God? I do not think so. It is plain that Jesus stayed in regular contact with God as he understood God and how to enrich that contact. Jesus certainly felt he was doing God's work as he went up and down the hills of Galilee preaching, teaching, and healing.

"Belief" in God has come in for an incredible amount of thought and discussion in recent centuries. Some historians and politicians have asserted that no avowed agnostic or atheist could be elected president of the United States. President Trump's election calls that hunch into serious question. He was elected by people who apparently cared not that he seemingly lacked both a religious practice and a moral compass. For many of us, notions of belief in/about God constantly change. As we moderns have learned more about the universe in which we live, we have generally come to see that there is no up and no down. Upness and downness are all around us; we exist in upness and downness. God up in heaven doesn't work very well, except maybe at some funerals when someone would eulogize that Papa is up there looking down on the funeral gathering. To go up to heaven or down to hell has little currency for most moderns. A possible and painful exception emerges as some religious barbarians are willing to blow themselves up (and innocent people around them). These terrorists claim to believe that such a death sends them immediately to a beatific version of heaven. Doing a bit of fact-checking on this notion, my favorite imam tells me this is a perversion of the overriding message of the Koran. What if there is nothing out there for these religious terrorists? What a horrible waste of human life.

In a freewheeling teenage confirmation class at our church a couple years ago, one of the young people said, "I don't believe in God."

"Tell me about the God in which you no longer believe," I suggested.

She proceeded to describe the God of vengeance, the capricious deity up in the sky who pulls strings over which humans have no control. When she had finished her discourse, I said, "Hey, I don't believe in that God either."

As I have said, in recent years I have puzzled over my own understanding of God. I affirm a sense of providence, a working out of a grand, cosmic, yet infinitely personal plan. Any notion of God, like every other human endeavor, is a creature of prisoner and promise of language. We humans are creatures of language. So the best we can do with any of this God talk is encapsulate it in language. At the same time, we know that our most profound feelings, hopes, and dreams go beyond language. That's why we keep talking, writing, drawing, inventing, sailing on the sea of faith. Poetry and imagination.

CHAPTER SIX

A Faithing Journey

Journey is a favorite and workable metaphor for anyone's life. We begin as infants, grow, and develop. We move from dependence to relative independence, and then if we live long enough, we return to some measure of interdependence or dependence. We learn, employ what we learn, then go into various stages of unlearning or forgetting. For a bit I want to frame a slice of the larger venture of my life so far as a faithing journey. Not a journey of faith. That would be presumptuous, suggesting that my eighty years have always been marked by faith. I have been and still am on an unfolding, ever-opening, boundaryless faithing journey.

We have highs and lows, successes and failures. We know joy and sorrow, health and decline. My personal faithing journey has included all these pieces. At eighty I begin to sense a movement through simple modalities made necessary by the growing-up and aging process that move me to more purpose, deliberation, and liberation. I cannot mark only one distinct "Aha!" moment. I have had several axial cluster moments that collectively have proven transformative. This third act space in my life becomes a time of gathering up, a time of assessment on the previous decades of my journey. This is also an opportunity to help move my life forward, unfold with purpose, clarity, more under my control. At the same time, as the years go by, I am aware the time may come when I have less control over both mind and body. I could regress to childhood physically and spiritually. The study of the biographies of notable women and men often points to pivotal moments. Those critical moments do not mark a halt to growth and change. They do mark turns in the road. For me this space serves only to point me to yet untraveled aspects of my own journey, to more of the "road less traveled."

George Washington seems to have channeled his bent for personal honor and glory, leading both the Revolutionary army and ultimately the aborning nation. Courage demonstrated in less than stunning military engagements surfaced personal inclusive insights to realize he had the courage and wisdom to lead an army and nation in the face of fierce and daunting battles. Twenty years later, that developed sense of honor abetted by his standing as a very wealthy Virginia landowner (and slaveholder) undergirded by this sense of courage put him in the position to lead the Continental Army. As a young Virginia militia officer the French and Indian War (1754–1763) set his face toward generalship in the Continental Army. Such a thought would have been unfathomable, not to say treasonable, as he slogged his way through the Virginia wilderness as a young colonial officer at the forefront of some raw troops while bullets zipped by him, tearing at his coat and killing his horse. But he was undoubtedly on a journey increasingly marked by a sense of purpose and direction. Each segment of the journey prepared him for the next segment. That's my story on a much less grand scale.

As I poke around in my psyche, I discern an upward curve in my willing-ness—actually eagerness—to push ahead. Where did this sense of adventure begin, this measure of existential confidence come from, whence my willing-ness to live with a plethora of ambiguities? What is my earliest memory of self? Where did I begin to differentiate myself from my surroundings? What is the genesis of the religious ethos that has always framed my life?

So a journey—as a person, husband, father, friend, minister, writer, politi-cal activist, and Jesus person—a faith journey, or a journey of faithing it. This is not an autobiography. It is a memoir—a selective telling of my story—and more to the point an effort for me to understand the faithing journey in which I have been engaged for these decades. This is not an attempt at systematic theology. It is a running memoir. The bits and pieces of the journey can be instructive as I discern contributing elements of the overall journey to my faithing perspec-tive. As I have indicated, this odyssey where I am today builds on all that has gone before, good and not so good, enlightening and mind-numbing. I am the product of layers of tradition, some I can describe, most beyond knowing. Countless familial, emotional, and tutorial tributaries have flowed together to set me on my journey, on my own "sea of faith," and bring me to this present juncture. For sure, you see I am the product of all that has gone before. Yet, like you, I am far more than the sum of all my parts.

So a faithing journey.

I have a fleeting, warm-and-fuzzy notion of myself as a child of three or four. I was in the suburban Atlanta Clarkston Baptist Church building in something I would later know as Sunday school. The door of the building was open, facing out toward a railroad track. While doing whatever I was doing, a train clattered by on the tracks. The moment holds comfortable, easy memories for me.

Fast forward a couple years when our family of four moved from Georgia to Norfolk and Portsmouth, Virginia, when my father went to work in the U.S. Navy Yard, building ships for World War II. Church and religion were practically absent from our home life during those war years. My father worked all the time in the Navy Yard. Twin brothers were born, now making us a household of four sons. In one of our several relocations around the greater Portsmouth/Norfolk region during those tumultuous years, we moved to a large apartment complex thrown together by the U.S. government to provide housing for the thousands of people who had poured into the area to do defense work.

While living there I started school at Cradock Elementary, Cradock, Virginia, a suburb of Portsmouth. In a community center located in the middle of the housing complex, a church group held a weeklong Vacation Bible School. I remember attending, I guess, alone. I may have been seven or eight years old. In keeping with evangelical religious custom, as the week ended the leaders held a "come to Jesus" service. That is, someone in authority invited the children to accept Jesus as savior and be baptized. Much is fuzzy, but I certainly wanted "Jesus in my heart," so I "went forward." When the preacher urged baptism on me, I remember responding, "I am not ready to do that." I would be thirteen before I was baptized and then only with a decided measure of adolescent reluctance.

In the midst of the tumult of war, we moved yet again, back to Norfolk, meaning I attended three schools in third grade. One day, in the second of those schools, the teacher asked the students what they wanted to be when they grew up. When my turn came, from somewhere down in my young, ill-formed psyche, I said I wanted to be a preacher. To this day I have no idea where that notion came from. We had no preachers in our family. Other than the brief time in the Vacation Bible School in the housing project, I had little involvement in religion. When some in the class giggled, I decided to keep that idea tucked away in my brain until a later day. I would be nineteen and a freshman in college before I declared for the ministry.

We moved yet again, this time back to Portsmouth, where I entered and finished fourth grade. At that time I began to attend regularly a neighborhood Baptist church alone. I remember few details except that I felt comfortable in the church environment.

A couple years after the war ended, my parents moved us back to Georgia. We initially settled in Lithonia, a small town six or eight miles east of Atlanta. As I have previously stated, during an early Billy Graham crusade in Atlanta, my parents made serious and life-changing spiritual dedications. Overnight, our family religious life moved up several notches. When Jesus really came into our home, I was an impressionable young teenager with a bundle of insecurities. This new fervor on the part of my parents, especially in my father, threw me into subterranean spasms of mortification. Whatever he did, he always did with abandon. His newfound religion was no exception. I cringed when he prayed out loud or read the Bible. He had little formal education, so his diction and thought patterns were jumbled to say the least. He could read, of course, but he could not read aloud very well. But he was a supremely courageous man, so he charged ahead with a full head of Billy Graham-fueled steam, and he never let up until the day he died. He worked, loved, laughed and taught us how to do the same.

I have come to appreciate that my father never met a task he could not master. He grew up on the outer edge of Atlanta on a small farm. His father— my grandfather, Maddox, of whom I was terrified—was a hard-drinking, cussing railroad man. As the Great Depression bore down, my parents met and married in 1931, secretly, to keep their jobs at the same place. I was not born until 1937 after my mother underwent "female" surgery.

In 1938 a friend gave my parents a small, vacant lot in Clarkston. With his innate skill as a builder and mechanic, my father set about to build us a house. We were living in that house when World War II broke out, whereupon he moved us to Virginia. During the war years, for some reason, my parents sold the house but kept ties in Clarkston. In 1950 my parents managed to build a new house near Clarkston, moving us (again) from the trouble-fraught Lithonia farm they had bought as a last resort when we relocated back in Georgia. In the very midst of moving into our new and, for the times, splendid house, my father made his complete career change from tradesman to traveling salesman.

These were my high school years, Clarkston High School and one year at Gordon Military College. Clarkston Baptist Church held forth as a completely unremarkable Southern Baptist church of that era. The preachers came and went, only one of whom made any impact on me as far as I can tell. In those early television and few automobile days, the church became the center of our family's religious and social life. My parents, especially my father, plunged into the full life of the congregation.

In those easy days of Southern Baptist life, before the denomination got embroiled in the ugly doctrinal fights of the late 1970s and into the 1980s, the church and denomination had much to offer families like ours. Sunday morning, we went to Sunday school and traditional worship. Sunday evenings, we took part in the Baptist Training Union and more informal worship time. During Sunday school we children—boys in one room and girls in another— were supposed to sit still and listen to the Bible lesson and go to the auditorium (no sanctuary or crosses for Baptists in those days; such were too Catholic!) and listen to the preacher. Sunday evening Training Union was different. Here, we gathered in coed groups. As I have previously mentioned, under the guidance of long-suffering leaders, the children gave the program. The national Southern Baptist Training Union office provided a curriculum that aimed to equip us to live the Christian life every day. I have long forgotten most of the lessons. What I do remember to this day is the leader's encouragement to study our "parts" ahead of time and then give them without reading from the booklet. Here, for the first time, I learned that I liked to hear myself talk.

With some regularity the youth Training Union spoke to the congregation in the evening service. Here again, I jumped at the chance to say something to the entire church. Public speaking proved to be a piece of cake for me. I have no memory of anything I said, but I still revel in the feeling of saying something to an audience.

As I mentioned earlier, beginning in tenth grade a few of my church friends who were also classmates at Clarkston High School became involved in the Atlanta YFC organization. Gradually, at their invitation, now with my own driver's license, I began to attend the regular Saturday evening rallies held in an Atlanta school auditorium. The preaching was tough. The leader always made a strong pitch for us to live "separated" lives from the evil world around us. Separation involved not going to movies and not dancing and behaving honorably with the opposite sex. The preaching always involved a strong call to trust Jesus as savior so one could avoid hell and go to heaven upon death.

As was the custom in Baptist churches, our local preacher always concluded his sermon with an invitation to accept Jesus as savior, join the church, and be baptized. He talked about heaven and hell but never with the intensity of the YFC preacher.

At the conclusion of the sermon at that first Saturday night rally I attended, the preacher told us to bow our heads and shut our eyes. Then the preacher fervently admonished us to be saved and accept Jesus and live the separated life. With every eye closed, if we wanted to be saved, we should raise our hand. Not stopping there, he urged us that if we were sure we were saved, we were to raise our hand, still keeping our eyes closed. Peeping, I saw many hands raised, so I put mine up also. After all, I had done everything I knew to do be saved and go to heaven when I died. I had told Jesus many times to come into my heart, though I was never sure he really did. I had been baptized in those cold waters of the Lithonia Baptist Church baptismal tank under a big lid up on the platform near the pulpit. I attended church regularly and basically liked going. So I was saved by all lights.

The preacher was not done yet. He asked us if we were saved but not satisfied with our lives as Christians to raise our hands. I knew I had a long way to go to measure up to the demands of the dedicated Christian life (I liked to go to movies and was not opposed to dancing), so I raised my hand. Then we were told to open our eyes. All who wanted to be saved should come down. Several young people responded. I breathed a sigh of relief since I had already, with some misgivings, assured myself I was saved. Now came the catch: "All those who raised your hand to live a better life should come down to the front, confessing your sins, and let me pray with you," the eager, young YFC leader admonished. Whoa! No way was I going to traipse down to the front and have this nice but intense super-Christian man pray over me. It had taken me two years to get the courage to go forward for baptism in our local church before family and friends who knew me. I was not about to bare my soul before a room full of people I did not know, with the exception of the four or five of my friends who were YFC regulars. Thereafter, I did attend the rallies fairly often, but I never again raised my hand in a rally.

We were also supposed to witness to our faith with fellow classmates, convincing them of their lostness before God, and invite them to accept Jesus and be saved so they too could go to heaven when they died. In those simpler days YFC could drive its beat-up bus onto the school campus and hold afterhours sessions in witness training. I attended one of those bus meetings. Number one, I simply could not do that sort of witnessing. I did not know why. I felt guilty. I just knew a friend of mine would spend an eternity in hell, lost and condemned because I did not confront him with the gospel and demand that he be saved. Still, it was just not part of me to do that. I had a visceral reaction to the whole blunt approach to witnessing. I was very fond of my friends who were buying the YFC message completely. I wanted to be with them and emulate them; I just could not comply with the practice. Fortunately, I soon got an afterschool job in a local grocery store, so I had a good excuse not to attend the bus sessions.

In my junior year of high school, my parents arranged for me to attend the nearby boarding Gordon Military College, both the town high school and a junior college. My local high school by any measure lacked a whole lot, making it woefully weak. I reveled in school work and made excellent grades with little effort. Gordon provided a new way of life: fun, military discipline, new friends, and excellent academics. After learning how to march, even marching to church, a mandatory part of the program, and handle an M1 rifle, I had a great time at the school. On occasion, when I was home on weekends, I would attend the YFC rallies more to be with friends and to be accepted by them than with any expectation of enlightenment.

For my senior year I returned to Clarkston High School and began dating a terrific classmate. We attended the rallies with some regularity. We did decide not to go to movies and not to attend school dances as the YFC preacher constantly exhorted. Instead, we had a great time going to concerts, including the symphony and, for both of us, our first opera. She decided to attend nursing school in Atlanta, and I chose Baylor University in Waco, Texas, so we parted ways, a painful but necessary separation.

Assessment
As I head into a major transition point, I pause and assess those first eighteen years (eight of which I can reasonably recall, from approximately age ten

until eighteen). I am grateful for the positive aspects of those formative years. Three years on the eighty-five-acre farm convinced me I did not want to be a farmer. At the same time, my brothers, some neighbor kids, and I discovered high adventure of life in the "vast and primitive" forests and native rock outcroppings behind our house. I could not have asked for more supportive parents. They were busy making a new life after the agonies of World War II. Looking back, I really do not have a clear idea of what they went through, absorbed as I was in my own adolescence. While we lived in the country, I do know they both worked in Atlanta, getting up early, before my brothers and me, and commuting into the city. I do not remember any breakfasts with them during the week. In fact, I don't remember very many meals together.

My maternal grandmother, Big Mama Causey, lived with us in the two-bedroom farmhouse on a dirt road about two miles from nearby Lithonia. The younger brothers slept in my parents' bedroom. My brother Mike and I slept on bunk beds in the same room with my grandmother. When they bought the farmhouse, we had only an outdoor privy. My father had never built a bathroom, but we needed one, so he built it on the back side of the house. We had maddening water problems with the well, our only source of water, constantly going dry. He solved that problem by regularly driving a huge old dump truck loaded with four or five fifty-five-gallon barrels into town to a friend's faucet. He would fill up the drums, drive back into the country, and then siphon the water from the barrels into the well. Efforts at a new well failed. We became active in the local Lithonia Baptist Church, where I was baptized at thirteen.

After three years of country-living hassle, he and Mother managed to build us the new house near Clarkston, back to our pre-war stomping grounds. This new house had three large bedrooms, a living room, dining room, large kitchen, and one and a half bathrooms with dependably flowing DeKalb County water. My grandmother moved with us. She had her own bedroom, and the four of us boys shared the other bedroom on bunk beds. We were in high cotton.

In the midst of this move came the high-risk decision that my father would become a traveling janitorial supply salesman to the then-thriving textile mills that made the southwest quadrant of Georgia hum with prosperity. Schools also became a major customer for him. To sell the supplies to the schools, he would often agree to strip and refinish the floors of the gymnasiums and cafeterias. This meant my brothers and I spent many hours mopping, stripping, and applying new finishes to these large open spaces. Daddy compensated by taking us for lunches to his favorite hot dog dives scattered in Southwest Georgia. Great time and great hot dogs!

For the first two or three years of this travel regimen, he left early Monday mornings in our only car and did not return until late Friday afternoon. Mother caught a ride to the nearest bus stop so she could get to her job in downtown Atlanta at the Georgia Power Company, a job she loved. My younger brothers rode the school bus to their elementary school. Rain or shine, I pedaled my bicycle to Clarkston High School, about three miles away. We did not complain. We felt no sense of deprivation. That was just the way life was.

In short order my father began to get the hang of the job and do well. In time we had a second car. When I turned sixteen, I inherited the rapidly aging Buick that I then used to get Mother to the bus stop and me to school. Church was fun, if not especially invigorating. My parents took us and a small cadre of fellow church members to the wonderful Ridgecrest Baptist Assembly in the mountains of North Carolina near Asheville. I can only thank Baptists of that era and God for providing such a grand place. Each week during the summer, thousands of us would gather for a week of fun, new friends, and all manner of Christian training events. There, for the first time, I heard preaching and music that moved me. At Ridgecrest I decided to someday earn a doctorate degree so I could be like a couple of the especially bright young leaders introduced as Dr. Jones or Dr. Perry who talked to us young people. Off and on for about fifteen years, I went to Ridgecrest and even three times to the brand new Glorieta Baptist Assembly in New Mexico. On several occasions after Linda and I married, we were invited to lead small groups at Ridgecrest, by then part of my life as a young Baptist minister.

Though the YFC brand of religion made me uncomfortable, the demanding call to Christian living entered my religious psyche. The rallies and super sell at least gave me something to react against, whereas regular participation in the local Baptist church would have soon become too bland to hold my attention. And always during my teen years I experienced the steady drumbeat in the inner recesses of my soul that I should be a minister. At Ridgecrest and in our steady dose of revival meetings in the local church, I would sometimes "go forward" during the cajoling invitation to "rededicate" my life to God, but I never went so far as to say I was answering a "call" to become a preacher. That was a huge step I was not ready to take.

In summer 1955 our family took the one big trip of our lives together. My parents decided we would journey from Georgia to the marvelous Glorieta Baptist Assembly near Santa Fe, New Mexico, see all we could of the country coming and going, and spend a week in Christian discipleship training. In order to save money, my father decided we would camp out along the way. Other than Boy Scout camps in safe and dry places, we had never camped out. No matter. Remember when we needed a bathroom on the farmhouse, so my father built a bathroom? No matter that we had never camped. We would camp. He borrowed an ugly open trailer we hitched to our new 1955 un-air-conditioned Chevrolet station wagon and loaded it with all manner of camping equipment, most of which we had never seen much less knew how to use. Well, we camped out two nights of the three-week excursion, but that's another story. We stayed in a series of old fashioned tourist courts—another story. He looked for the sign that read, "Clean, Modern Tourist Court." Invariably, the place was neither clean nor modern. On our way back we did stop one night in a new motel somewhere that was air-conditioned and had a swimming pool. It was a cash-only trip in the era before credit cards. A time or two my father hinted that our money might be running low, filling me with panic, lest we run out of funds in the middle of nowhere. Fortunately, we made it home with, I suppose, some money left over.

The point is that during the week at Glorieta, I met that fun gang of young people who were entering Baylor University that fall. Though my mother had enrolled me in an Atlanta college, determined I would start college somewhere in the fall, I decided on Baylor, though I had never been in Texas, much less seen the school in Waco.

They agreed, relieved that I had found my place. By then it was mid-July. In those days before SATs and heavy entrance requirements, I called the registrar and was immediately admitted. About three weeks before departure, I dropped by Lawson Jolly's house. Though two years ahead of me, he had bounced around and was not really settled into a school. "Go with me to Baylor," I suggested. To my utter amazement and delight he paused a minute, looked at me, and said, "Okay. Let's do it."

A phone call later, and he was admitted. We got on the train in Atlanta and rode endlessly until we arrived three days later in Waco on an incredibly hot and steamy September afternoon. We were met by Mother Russell, who ran an off-campus rooming house for Baylor men, who after another phone call had agreed to take us in. I fell in love with the school instantly. Though I had no idea what I had wanted in a college, Baylor had it all. I immediately linked up with friends I had met at Glorieta and began four deliriously productive, happy years.

Still not willing to admit my sense of call to ministry, I signed up for a pre-med course, including chemistry, zoology, and trigonometry, none of which I had ever had in high school. I scraped by in math and biology but flunked chemistry in fine fashion—two Cs and an F, my first failure in over twelve years of school, not an especially auspicious beginning to my college career. I must have written home about my failing chemistry grade. From out of the blue, my mother paged me one day in the school's student union. Fearing something bad had happened, I rushed to the phone. "Why don't you just pack up and come home," she said. "You've never failed anything in your life. If Baylor is too much, just leave."

"Come home? Mother, the thought never entered my mind. I'll do better next time." And I did.

Next term, I changed my major and took English, history, and New Testament and earned two As and a B and an invitation to become a grader for the history professor. That spring, on a Sunday night in our invigorating campus church, Seventh and James Baptist Church, I "went forward" at the standard invitation and told the minister, the able and brilliant Charles Wellborn, that I was "surrendering" to the ministry. Back in the dorm later, my roommate said, "What took you so long?"

I had never studied New Testament, though I had been in Sunday school for the past eight or nine years. I loved the course and the professor, Dr. Yandall Woodfin. The class prompted the first of many serendipitous blips of fresh, albeit discomforting, enlightenment. Seated in the rather deep chill of the new, air-conditioned Tidwell Bible Building library studying for a test, maybe my first big New Testament test, the thought flashed across my young, highly impressionable mind, "What does something like the resurrection of Jesus 2,000 years ago really have to do with my life in 1956?"

Hmm. Interesting thought. It was quite a moment, but I tucked it away in my mind to tend to later at a more opportune time.

As my biblical and theological education unfolded across the next twenty years through college, seminary, and then doctoral studies, that freshman question stayed with me. As time went on and my education and exposure broadened, I began to be increasingly suspicious that the resurrection of Jesus 2,000 years ago really had nothing directly to do with my life in the twentieth century. I could believe it as a fact in my head. But that is about as far as the resurrection of Jesus went with me. Still, I had almost nothing with which to address the persistent question.

Whereas I enjoyed Baylor University, most of the religion courses I took, now as a ministerial student, held little charm for me. I had some truly first-class English, history, and philosophy courses and a few fairly stimulating theology courses. Few straight Bible courses gave me a buzz. Baylor, no doubt, had some able religion professors. As I have suggested, I know now that they taught within the Texas/Southern Baptist theological culture that asked very few serious questions of Baptist theology and never wandered off into the creative or remotely ground-breaking territory that was challenging the larger theological and academic post-World War II world. I did not know where the new knowledge was, not in college or seminary. I just began to have the gnawing hunch there was more I was missing. No problem. I was having fun, making many friends, falling in love with Linda Cook, who had transferred to Baylor at the beginning of her sophomore year, and holding places of leadership in campus life to give much serious thought to the new information that was bound to be out there.

Real stimulation came from the vibrant religious life of the Baylor campus in those years. We held a weekly student-run Baylor Religious Hour on Wednesday nights in the main school auditorium. We heard some truly notable preachers, including the inimitable and irascible Dr. Carlyle Marney, iconoclastic pastor from the First Baptist Church of Austin, Texas. What a mind and spirit! The Rev. Bill Lawson, a marvelously gifted African-American pastor from Houston, preached with some regularity. More than anyone else, Bill Lawson began to open my mind to the terrible racial injustices that afflicted national and especially southern life in those years. Baylor was lily white, and we never gave it a thought until Bill Lawson, with his quiet, poetic brilliance, made his way into my heart and mind. And, as recalled earlier, I will forever be indebted to Charles Wellborn, pastor of our Seventh and James Baptist Church right across the street from the campus. With him in the pulpit and Dr. Euell Porter leading the choir and music, every Sunday was an energizing worship adventure.

Two weeks after my graduation in May 1959, Linda and I married in her hometown, which had become my hometown thanks to my parents' move (ah, how many moves?) from Atlanta to Thomaston, Georgia, when I was a Baylor sophomore. We returned to Baylor for her to complete her senior year. I worked with George Cowden in the Baptist Student Union and became the part-time youth director in a local Baptist church.

By the time of her graduation in May 1960, Linda was pregnant. In those days a woman could not teach school while pregnant. To complete her practice teaching at a Waco high school without revealing her "condition," Linda had to wear bulkier clothes toward the end of the semester while she completed her required stint in the classroom. Both sets of parents drove out from Georgia for her graduation. With my contract at the university expiring and no job prospects, my father, in his inimitable way, packed all our worldly goods in a U-Haul trailer and prepared for us to move back to Georgia. Because of his years traveling through Southwest Georgia, he knew scores of preachers and deacons. He had arranged for me to preach in a lovely little church in a village not far from Thomaston. We would have our baby, and I would find a way to attend seminary somewhere in Atlanta or move to Louisville and study at the then-venerable Southern Baptist Theological Seminary.

Literally at the last minute, a day before we were to head to Georgia, by the grace of God, I was offered a position at the huge First Baptist Church of Arlington, Texas, only fifteen miles from Fort Worth and the large Southwestern Baptist Theological Seminary. I readily, gratefully accepted the position, and after a few days' visit back in Thomaston, we moved to Arlington for me to serve as youth director. Frankly, I was not excited about studying at Southwestern, but the situation was too fortuitous for me to turn down.

We settled in and had a rollicking summer with the hundreds of teenagers in the church. We made friends who have endured across the decades.

In the fall of 1960, with Linda nearing delivery, I began my studies in Fort Worth, commuting daily with others in the church and town who, likewise, were studying at the seminary. With all their failings in recent years, Southern Baptists provided well for seminarians. I paid only $100 a semester for a full load at Southwestern.

From my earliest days at Baylor, harking back to those teenage days at Ridgecrest Assembly, I had determined that sooner or later, one way or another, I would obtain that doctor's degree in something. The seminary was highly competitive for the chance to pursue a doctorate after completing the basic degree, then the bachelor of divinity, later renamed the master of divinity. To stay in the running for eventual doctoral work, one had to have practically all As. My first Greek test came the day our son, Andy, was born. By the time I took the makeup exam, it became quite clear that Greek was not my best subject. "B" on that first test essentially doomed my pursuit of a higher degree at Southwestern. I accepted my fate with equanimity (maybe with existential confidence?), not especially fazed by the ambiguity of thwarted plans. In retrospect I realize that almost from the first day in that seminary, I sensed the school held only minimal charm for me.

That first semester I took a light load and finished with good grades. I also calculated that if I took a light load each semester, it would take me a long time to finish. The next semester, I took a full load, did my work quite well at the church, moved into fatherhood and married life, and still managed to pull off good grades. I finished school in three years, plus one short summer school session that allowed me to complete my Hebrew requirement.

What I did off campus had as much, if not more, impact than class work. I discovered I had a genuine knack for church work. I had two able mentors. Tilson Maynard was pastor of the Waco neighborhood church I served as youth director that year while Linda finished. I made my first solo pastoral hospital visit after tagging along with him on a run or two. I helped in my first funeral. Was that an episode! An older father had died. In her howling grief one of his adult daughters actually tried to crawl over into the open casket where her dead father lay. Henard East had served as pastor of the church in Arlington for many years when I joined the staff. He had taken the church before he even finished college with no seminary training. By love, compassion, able if not charismatic preaching, and pounds of shoe leather, he had seen it become a congregation of 2,500 members. I watched him and learned. He blessed me even though he gave little hands-on advice.

As youth minister I led a cadre of the older teens to do some fun but serious reading. We waded part of the way through Dietrich Bonhoeffer's *The Cost of Discipleship*. A publisher had produced a series of smaller books reflecting work of top scholars of the time. Of best memory is *The Existentialist Posture* by Roger Shinn. Thereafter, to this day, I regard myself as a Christian existentialist. Such a small book has had enduring echoes in my personal and ministerial life. Talking a few years ago with a couple of my "teenagers," they likewise remember Shinn's paperback book and the impact it made on them.

I took away from the seminary a growing if, as yet, ill-formed disaffection with the preacher culture that controlled Southern Baptist life. My best friends in the seminary shared the same distaste. Rather than attending the daily chapel services where a variety of male current bright lights held forth, we preferred to remain in the basement coffee shop. By decree of the school's president, we could not buy coffee while chapel took place upstairs. And the manager had to turn off most of the lights in the cafe. Okay, so we were just as arrogant in our way as the preachers upstairs, but we made our point, though no one but us noticed or cared.

Only when I began preparation for the graduate theological examination to begin doctoral work at Candler School of Theology of Emory University in 1968 did I confront what I had missed of prevailing academic theological scholarship. At any rate I had to pay a huge price of hard study to get ready for the big test. I passed by the grace God.

Linda and I made lifelong friends with some of the people from First Baptist Church, Arlington, Texas, including Louise and Roy Wood and their children, Mary Ann and Joe. George and Jean Hawkes and their clan likewise took their place in our hall-of-fame friends. George and John Gaston and Tony Martin have remained warm and important friends.

Upon graduating from the seminary in summer 1963, I accepted a call to become an associate pastor at the North Jacksonville (Florida) Baptist Church, where the father of one of our best college friends was the pastor. According to Southern Baptist polity at the time, the local church, my own First Baptist of Arlington, ordained me to the ministry in a service attended by our parents and a good host of friends. We moved to Jacksonville in August 1963. Again, we made good friends, had success as a developing minister, but basically were not comfortable in the church's ugly systemic racism and hyper-growth culture.

On one of our trips home to Georgia during seminary, my father connected me with the inimitable Rev. Clinton Cutts, pastor of the First Baptist Church of Vienna, Georgia.[8] Rev. Cutts took me on a quick tour of the stately "Akron"-style church building. He had grown up in this small South Georgia town at the turn of the 20th century while his father served as pastor of the church. These years later, he had returned to Vienna as the pastor in his own right. This canny, fun, gifted minister had led the church well, including a thorough renovation of the charming late-nineteenth-century sanctuary and educational space. Vienna was the home of the iconic Sen. Walter F. George, so Brother Cutts' penultimate building project involved the construction of the George Chapel within the footprint of the building. When Sen. George died in 1957, Brother Cutts conducted his funeral, which was attended by many Washington luminaries. The funeral guests signed a large red book the women of the church had enshrined in a glass cabinet at the door of the chapel. Prominent in the book was the signature of Lyndon Baines Johnson, president of the United States by the time we moved to Vienna.

From the moment I walked through the buildings with Brother Cutts, I was smitten with the idea of becoming pastor of the church upon his impending retirement. By the summer of 1964 Brother Cutts had decided to retire and remain in the town where he had built himself a new house. Again, through his auspices and with a bit of help from my father, who knew some members of the pastor search committee, Linda and I were invited to come for the "trial" sermon in October 1964. We drove the four or five hours from Jacksonville to Vienna to meet the church and offer a sermon for which I have no ounce of recall. To our amazement when I had finished my sermon, Mr. Stone (another of my all-time favorite people), the chairman of the search committee, invited Linda and me to step into the pastor's office at the rear of the sanctuary, a request that puzzled us a bit. To my utter surprise and delight, within a few minutes Mr. Stone came to the study and announced that the church had just called me as the new pastor! I was flabbergasted, but of course I said yes. On our way back to Jacksonville, Linda asked me, "What's your salary?" I had no idea. But I was pastor of the First Baptist Church of Vienna, Georgia.

Linda, Andy, and I moved to the church and town in November 1964 and began a four-year journey with the grand people of Vienna, Dooly County, Georgia, one of the major cotton- and peanut-producing regions of the state. No young minister could have been given a better place to start. Our second son, Ben, was born while we lived there. I discovered solid gifts as a pastor, learned a great deal about preaching, and, maybe most of all, listened to and learned from Brother Cutts. For instance, as I began, he came by one day and reminded me that he would remain in the town as a resident but would never give me a minute's trouble. He assured me of his support and his readiness to offer suggestions when called upon. Then he said something like, "Bob, if you will love the people, they will love you. Take care of them, and they will take care of you. They will walk with you through the ups and downs of your ministry here." No better advice could come to a new and, upon later reflection, very green minister.

Recall that this was the 1960s, an era of great upheaval in our country. President Kennedy had been murdered just a year before our move to Vienna. Martin Luther King Jr. and the civil rights movement surged in full tilt. While we were there, the Vietnam War heated up to boiling point. President Johnson had persuaded Congress to pass the Voting Rights Act and the Public Accommodation Act, both of which struck at the heart of ugly segregation in the South, posing profound threats to the deeply entrenched segregation culture that had blighted the South since the Civil War. It looked indeed like the "center would not hold." The nation seemed to be coming apart at the seams.

My own civil rights consciousness had evolved slowly but steadily. As I have noted, in my years at Baylor we had no students of color, but I hardly noticed. For the waning days of the 1950s, other than the powerful, unsettling occasional preaching of Rev. Bill Lawson, Baylor paid little attention to national politics, including the steady drumbeat of Martin Luther King Jr. and his minions. During my final year at seminary, I took Christian ethics from Dr. T. B. Maston, one of the truly world-class ethics scholars anywhere. Despite the near total antipathy of the seminary's president and the prevailing Texas Baptist culture, Dr. Maston kept the flag of social justice and civil rights flying high. He retired as I graduated. Rumor was that the seminary president disliked him so intently that, unlike other retired professors who kept teaching beyond the contract age, Dr. Maston was never invited back to the seminary. His message, however, took root in a generation of great Baptist civil rights leaders such as James Dunn, Foy Valentine, and Jimmy Allen, who took turns leading Texas Baptists and then Southern Baptists, albeit kicking and screaming, into the thick of the civil rights movement.

I surmise now that those fuzzy years in college, seminary, and Jacksonville prepared me somewhat for the pervasive racism in Vienna. Fortunately, I had acquired sufficient pastoral skills from my mentors that enabled me to wend my way through the thicket of prejudice and injustice in church and town to exert a measure of leverage and still not get fired. Stories abound that need to be told in another venue of preachers from other nearby towns who did get fired for making efforts at racial reconciliation.

A few pieces of those years in South Georgia do stand out. With Martin Luther King Jr. marching in Alabama and even nearby Albany, Georgia, Brother Cutts, the Methodist minister, and a leading black minister decided I needed to be chairman of the *ad hoc* racial reconciliation committee. With a bit of fear and trembling, I thanked them for offering me up on the altar of justice. The committee never met, but the presence of such a group made up of white and black preachers maybe defused what could have been a volatile climate.

As I prepared to leave Vienna after four years and enter graduate school at Emory University, Napoleon Williams, the town's leader of the black community, a minister and the principal of the segregated school, asked me to come to his office. In one of the more memorable conversations I have ever had, he said, "I always wanted to come to your church to hear you preach, but I could not. You have preached in some of our churches, but I could not go to yours." He went on to say, "I could attend funerals and maybe a wedding in your church, but only if I came in after the service began and sat on the back row." He reminded me that black people who worked for white people knew all about "us." The maids, farmhands, and janitors knew who was running around on their spouses, whose teenage daughter was pregnant and by which football player, which of the families was in deep financial trouble, etc. "We know all of that," he said, "but you know nothing of our community." With an ineffable sadness he said quietly, "And by and large the white people do not care what happens in our community." He thanked me for my efforts as pastor and town leader and wished me Godspeed as I embarked for graduate study. I went back to the church a few years later for the funeral of a prominent white citizen and spoke to Napoleon as he exited from his seat on the back row of the sanctuary.

When President Johnson instituted his Great Society/War on Poverty program, including Head Start for young, preschool children, someone in the town, maybe the beleaguered county school superintendent, asked Linda to head the local program. When word leaked out that she would take the point on Head Start, one of our best friends called to warn her that her leadership of the new program could cost me my job. We did not want to get fired like several other preachers in the area, but Linda, without a blink, moved ahead and launched Head Start.

During the Vienna days I began to push beyond my college and seminary education. I read two seminal books: *Honest to God* by John A. T. Robinson and *The Lliving of These Days* by Reverend Harry Emerson Fosdick. Both challenged me to my bones. The church provided some travel and convention money. Rather than use the funds to go to a round of traditional Baptist meetings, I decided on a different route. Linda's uncle, an esteemed Methodist minister in Georgia, suggested that I attend the pastors' week at Union Theological Seminary in New York City. Great idea! We had never gone to New York City. How we managed that trek is another of those stories for another time and place. The week, however, proved prescient. One of the major topics was "Am I My Fetus's Keeper?" Abortion was not remotely on the South Georgia radar. The sessions at Union served as an important early push to point me in hitherto undreamed of theological and social justice directions.

In about 1965 I attended my first Christian Life Seminar sponsored by the Southern Baptist Christian Life Commission led by Dr. Foy Valentine. This one met at Southern Baptist Theological Seminary in Louisville, Kentucky. For many years this inimitable, irascible, brutally honest, and courageous man led my former and lamentable Southern Baptist Convention through the national civil rights upheavals that tore at the soul of the nation, especially the South. For years Foy and his Christian Life Commission sponsored these annual seminars, forcing a small army of Baptist preachers and churches to take hard looks at ourselves. I ultimately attended several of these seminars. Invariably, I came away fortified and edified to face my own and cultural demons with more honesty and skill. I owe Dr. Valentine and his team a huge debt. No wonder hardly an annual circus-like meeting of the Southern Baptist

Convention occurred without some preacher proposing a resolution to at least censure, if not abolish, Foy's commission as an unnecessary burr under the convention's saddle. Fortunately, none passed.

By the time he retired, the Southern Baptist Convention had suffered a legal but tragic takeover by the most rigid fundamentalist wing of the organization. One of the first moves of the newly configured convention came when ultraconservative trustees abrogated everything that Dr. Valentine had undertaken. From then until most recently, that agency was essentially one of the major conservative religious voices for the Republican far right. Sad. I do say that under the leadership of Dr. Russell Moore, elected to the executive position in 2013 after a welcome shakeup, the newly minted organization has become somewhat more courageous and less the voice of the far-right wing of national politics.

I remember two aspects of that first Christian Life Seminar. We viewed and discussed the movie *Valley of the Dolls*, one of the early films about the burgeoning and increasingly deadly drug culture in America. The female star, Sharon Tate, was later brutally murdered by the Manson "family."

The second impact came from the late great Dr. Wayne Oates, who lectured on pastoral psychology, a field he helped pioneer. I can still remember some of his insights. All in all, I came away from that seminar pained by how much I did not know. At that same time what I heard whetted my appetite to keep at my real, still yet indistinct pursuits. That important freshman Bible student "so what?" historical question continued to roam around in my head: How much of past dogma did I need to cling to in order to live the Christian life in my time? Persistent, it was a gnawing rumble that became a benchmark for my developing faith outlook.

How would I chart this new direction for myself that flew in the face of the ethos in which I had grown up, encountered through years of Baptist church, university, and seminary? What if I was on the wrong track entirely? Would God cut me off? And what about climbing in the denomination? After all, the measure of professional success was bigger, more prestigious churches.

Grace. Where did I begin to embrace the charm, support, courage of grace? I do not recall. But looking back, I realize I had begun to consider grace in fresh ways. I came to internalize the grace of God, the generosity of God that would envelop me regardless of my decreasing attachment to traditional theological dogma.

Coursing through all the newness, I began to sense a new freedom, a virtual liberation to think and feel beyond what I had thought and felt before! Here again, that faithing-framed confidence coupled with little sleep lost over ambiguities kicked in, though at the time I was not using such language to describe my experiences. I pause to thank my anonymous ancestors for the gift of freedom-loving genes. I likewise thank Linda and a small cadre of like-minded friends for emotional bulwarks and important camaraderie.

Another *excursus*. The Vienna days proved important from another pivotal angle. During the Vienna days I first became acquainted with Jimmy Carter. Carter, a state senator from nearby Plains, Georgia, ran for governor in 1966 but lost. Thanks to a vote-siphoning third-party candidate, the super-clown politician, arch-segregationist Lester Maddox, no known kin, became governor. Having lost, Carter never stopped running. Twice in my four years, as I left for vacation, at my father's suggestion, I called Jimmy and asked him to supply preach for me. Word was out on the preacher gossip network that Carter would preach but did not accept an honorarium. I never actually met him face to face until after his 1970 gubernatorial election when he came for a visit to Atlanta's Druid Hills Baptist Church, where by then I was associate pastor.

In addition, Jody Powell, who became one of the two most important advisors to Governor and then President Carter, hailed from Dooly County stock that reached back several generations. Soon after arriving in Vienna, Jody came to see me. He and his family in later years became close friends with Linda and me. When Jody died in 2009, I delivered one of the eulogies. Jody would ultimately play a significant role in enabling me to join the Carter White House staff in 1979. (Jimmy Carter and Jody Powell, though friends, would not become a significant part of our lives for yet a while.)

Another key piece of my political and social justice development came from unfailing absorption of Ralph McGill's blistering editorials in the *Atlanta Constitution* calling for racial justice in Georgia and the nation. I had never paid much attention to newspapers until I moved to Vienna, but that great newspaper became a key part of my daily routine. Of course, many in Georgia regularly consigned McGill to the pits of political and social hell, but he pushed me further down the road toward a growing pain and then outrage at the way we whites treated our black neighbors.

The news of Martin Luther King Jr.'s murder crashed through the state's, the nation's, and the world's psyche. Linda and I sat glued to our black-and-white television set. Brother Cutts alerted me to be alive to trouble in our town and county. Everyone remained calm, but even the whitest among us knew that something visceral in our lives had pulsed.

Tony Martin from the Arlington, Texas, church had finished high school, gone on to graduate from Baylor University, and had entered Southwestern Seminary. A warm and enduring friendship developed though we corresponded only occasionally. "Bob," he said on the phone, "I am coming to Atlanta to attend Dr. King's funeral. I want you to meet me at the airport and go with me."

I had not programmed that King's funeral would be in Atlanta, and I certainly had never thought of attending! Without a blink, however, I said, "Sure." Then, gaining resolve, "Of course. I will meet you at the airport. You can come here to Vienna for a day, and then we will head to Atlanta."

As Tony and I pulled out of the driveway to begin the three-hour drive to Atlanta, Linda said, "Bob, if you see a TV camera, get under it. Do not let yourself be filmed." Only then did the possible danger to my job such a venture posed dawn on me. We attended the funeral—actually, the long march from Ebenezer Church to Morehouse College campus where the public service was held. The night before, we had stood in line for hours, waiting our turn to pay our respects before the open casket of the slain civil rights leader, two white faces amidst thousands of dark ones.

Getting Tony to the plane and driving back to Vienna, I reflected on the power of the event with no real thought to any possible threats to my job. I am glad to report that even though news of my attendance at the funeral surely leaked out, no one objected. In fact, I pause here to laud the underlying grace of the people of the First Baptist Church as they tolerated, maybe even appreciated, my active dismay at our collective attitudes. Other than a few sideswipes at Linda and me, the congregation understood our deep concerns. Maybe even some of them shared those pains but lacked the leverage to let friends and family know of their feelings. For sure, threats of censure against us never arose.

After four happy years—if fraught with the usual vagaries of everyday life—in Vienna, I managed to put a deal together that allowed me to enroll in the Candler School of Theology at Emory University and begin work on the Doctor of Sacred Theology. In late summer 1968 we moved to Atlanta for me to embark on the Emory University program.

Jumping ahead, Linda and I were visiting with the Carters in Plains in summer 2017. With only twenty-five miles separating Plains and Vienna, we decided to ride over and take another look at where we had lived those many years ago (1964–1968). The church looked even better than it had in my years. At some point the congregation had added a family life center on the ground where the church's first parsonage had stood for decades. Sad to say the town itself had deteriorated like so many small towns throughout the nation. We rode by the "new" parsonage the church built during our years. It still looked as handsome and comfortable as ever. We talked with no one, but from the looks of the church's two properties, we were persuaded the congregation was doing well despite the decline in the town center. Memories flooded us again, along with profound gratitude for the grand start the people of town and church provided Linda and me and our family. Thank you, First Baptist Church, Vienna, Georgia.

In 1968 sadness at leaving was offset with the academic adventure that lay ahead. At last I would earn that longed-for doctorate. The seminary had tailored the degree for the person, primarily men at that time, who wanted to remain in active pastoral ministry but who desired serious further training by pursuing a full academic degree with a special pastoral focus. Thanks to the help of some good folks and initial income derived from selling pictorial church directories (all the rage at that time), we moved to Atlanta.

Selling pictorial church directories proved more daunting and less remunerative than I had anticipated. To supplement our skinny income, Linda and I, with the reluctant assistance of young Andy and Ben, spent several weeks delivering those huge yellow-page phonebooks to a large section of our part of town. By the grace of God, while pitching the idea of a pictorial directory to the historic Druid Hills Baptist Church in Atlanta, the recently installed pastor invited me to become his associate, a position I readily accepted. We loved the church and reveled in its history, especially our contact with the venerable

Dr. Louie Newton, "Mr. Baptist" of that era, who had led the church as pastor for nearly forty years. Though retired, he remained a force until his death at 92.

My five years at Candler School of Theology at Emory University opened a compelling, energized, broadened theological perspective and worldview to me. Here, at last, I began to match a persistent if ill-defined theological discomfort with scholarship that could fill in some of those gaps. I could assimilate learning that pointed me to answers or at least to approaches that made sense to me.

Reading for the required Graduate Theological Examination as the gateway to acceptance into the doctoral program, I encountered for the first time the likes of Paul Tillich and Rudolf Bultmann. Frankly, I absorbed more than I actually retained from these giants. Nonetheless, from them I took another step toward the emerging theological and ecclesiastical liberation.

I attended another of Foy Valentine's Christian Life Seminars, this one in New York City. When I called Linda from LaGuardia Airport to tell her the plane was late, she burst out laughing and crying over the phone: "I am pregnant!" What a homecoming! I was elated but also concerned, because her pregnancy with Ben had landed her in the hospital several times with ferocious nausea and awful kidney stones. To our great joy Elizabeth arrived in October 1971. Sure enough, it was a rough pregnancy.

Having completed the residency requirements for the degree, we needed to find a more settled ministry, both because I wanted to be the senior pastor again and because we needed more income, especially with three children. In the providence of God, First Baptist Church of Calhoun, Georgia, made overtures. We talked back and forth, met with the search committee, and then did the preaching weekend. I began my ministry in Calhoun, about seventy-five miles north of Atlanta, in October 1971. Linda was simply too sick with her pregnancy to make the move, so I set about to commute from Calhoun to our home east of Atlanta, about an hour and a half drive. Elizabeth was born October 23, and we moved during the Thanksgiving holidays. As we had Vienna and Druid Hills in Atlanta, we loved Calhoun and had a highly productive eight years.

Though I had completed my doctoral residency requirements, still I had three more huge academic hurdles before me. The degree required three months of full-time pastoral clinical training in a certified setting. No such framework existed around Calhoun, so I arranged with the church's leadership to let me commute to Georgia Baptist Hospital in Atlanta for the three months. Again, nothing I had ever done prepared me for the highs and lows of those three months. The Southwestern Baptist Seminary in Fort Worth made no such requirements. I waded off into the program without a clue of what clinical training was all about. A great boost to this effort came when Rev. J. W. Wallis, one of the local pastors, decided he would take the course on his own, so we commuted together for the three months, forming one of the most important friendships I have known. I worked very hard at being the new pastor while commuting five days a week. If the church felt any neglect, they did not let me know.

The next step required that I shape my doctoral project. In my degree program, rather than a research dissertation, the candidate had to develop a project that could enhance one's ministry and meet the high academic and professional standards the seminary had set. Almost from the first day in the program, I knew what I wanted to do—a project involving evangelism. The year I spent shaping the doctoral program proved both vexing and stimulating.

Southern Baptists of the twentieth century had all but gone to seed on church growth. Expansion of the church rolls called for people to join the local church by transfer of their membership from another like-minded Baptist church or by conversion from nothing or whatever a previous religious experience might have been to "faith in Jesus Christ as Lord and Savior and baptism by immersion."

When I reflect on my concern about evangelism, I hark back to my teenage YFC evangelism anxiety as well as the intense focus most Southern Baptist churches placed on evangelism by conversion. Evangelism in that genre was always focused on getting a person ready not to live in the faith but to die in the faith so one could avoid a burning hell and gain entrance into heaven. To be sure, most of the preachers urged moral living for the saved. But moral living was basically avoiding sins of the flesh. The preachers rarely emphasized the joy and adventure of living in a dynamic relationship with God as expressed in Jesus Christ.

Dr. Kenneth Chafin, a young and charismatic preacher and professor, taught evangelism classes at Southwestern Seminary. I liked him and greatly admired his ability. But through two of his courses I had to take, I became increasingly uncomfortable with his, and the prevailing Baptist approach, to evangelism and conversion. Years later, when I had gained a good measure of professional footing, and after he had left the seminary, I interacted with him about those courses and his approach. Though he never actually admitted his own ambivalence and the change of his own thinking over the years after the seminary, he let me know that he too had become uncomfortable with the almost robotic way of witnessing to a "lost" person and the rote way we baptized and then did little more to nurture the new life in the person.

Not for a long time had I believed to any significant degree in a burning, everlasting hell. Again, I had no tools with which to parse my ambiguity about hell. The fact that I could not preach a fiery hell also meant I could never win the prize for being able to report the most baptisms in my annual "letter" to the local Baptist organization. Still, what if it were true, and I did not work hard enough to save people from hell when they died? The years in residency at Candler enabled me to find the theological and personal freedom gradually to put aside the notion of a burning hell. That was quite a leap for me. But still I wanted people to come to a deep personal relationship with Jesus as Lord of life. Looking back, I did not have a clear idea of Jesus as Lord of life. The idea of working for justice for all humanity as a Jesus person would come later. Thus, during the year or so of preparing my doctoral project, I read extensively, talked with people I respected outside the mainstream of Southern Baptist life, and gradually developed my own idea of "evangelism without reference to eschatology." In that effort I disentangled evangelism and witnessing from the notion of heaven or hell. I began to say the life of faith, the walk with God in Jesus Christ, was worth the effort just because that quality of life had so much to offer. I was scared. I suffered considerable angst as that approach became more clearly defined in my mind. Not only was I challenging prevailing Baptist theology of evangelism; I was moving against a hallmark of Southern Baptist culture that focused the life of faith on dying rather than living.

"Fine," my adviser said after I had written and revised the project over and over again. The second hurdle: "What will be your method? You have to do this," he reminded me. How to do New Testament evangelism as I was coming to understand it?

I had the method already in mind.

In one of the earliest Christian Life Seminars I attended, Dr. Valentine had invited Rev. Gordon Cosby, pastor of the unique Church of the Savior in Washington, DC. At that time I was unaware of the long-lasting influence he would have on me. I had heard of Gordon Cosby and had read some of the books the church fostered (see the several books by Elizabeth O'Connor). As I mentioned earlier, he had come out of World War II as a chaplain intending to lead a Baptist church in his native Virginia. Quickly, however, he and his wife, Mary, realized they did not want to spend time in a traditional Baptist church, even a progressive one like they were involved with.

"Call to service" stood at the center of the church's approach to ministry. Under this rubric a specific thrust of service came from a sense of call from the Cosbys or someone connected to the Church of the Savior. These people, like Gordon and Mary, were on a "journey inward and a journey outward." Through prayer, worship, and shared community they opened themselves to the leadership of the Spirit to point them in ministry directions. For instance, a participant in the church would become persuaded that the Adams-Morgan section of Washington, DC, at that time a hard-pressed part of the city, needed a women's clinic to treat the underserved female population. He or she would pray, massage the idea, then begin talking with Gordon or Mary about their sense of call. After a further period of discernment, Gordon and the congregant would, as they said, sound a call to the larger faith community. All those who could share in that call would begin to coalesce around the concept. If no one responded to the call, typically Gordon would counsel patience. Keep praying, studying the need, doing spiritual due diligence, then maybe sound the call again.

This sense of called ministry brought into being some of the most salient, perceptive ministries in the city. In time the women's clinic, the fabled Potter's House Book and Coffee Shop, Jubilee Housing, the Ruth House, Dayspring, and more emerged. When the ministries had sufficient grounding and stability, often after years of serving the physical and social needs of a given segment of the population, the entity would spin off from the core church and become its own IRS-recognized nonprofit agency. Gordon did not want the Church of the Savior to become so institutionalized and bureaucratized that the movement of the Spirit of God would become thwarted.

A "called group" to spend time with me in studying and doing New Testament evangelism along the lines I was envisioning would be the method. I read more of the books that emerged from the church, especially the writings of Elizabeth O'Connor, who put in print the work of the church. I drove to Washington and spent the day with Gordon, who was warm, generous, encouraging, and affirming. Then, at his suggestion I spent a weekend at Dayspring in suburban Maryland, the retreat center that people in the church had felt called to establish. About twenty-five of us from around the country would spend two days in prayer and reflection and then, to my initial emotional panic, enter into silence for twenty-four hours. I had never been silent for twenty-four hours. After a few hours of grave discomfort, I moved into the silence and only with reluctance broke the silence the next day as we prepared to leave.

My graduate adviser, Dr. Frederick Prussner, also knew of the Church of the Savior and agreed for me to give the called group approach a try and see what happened. I wrote, prayed, thought, planned, and then, according to the outline of the project, wrote the entire congregation my hope that some of them could hear the call I would sound and join me in the journey. At an appointed Sunday I preached a sermon in which I sounded the call. "If you can hear this call, albeit fuzzy, contact me in the next few days." And then I waited. If no one responded, I had to start all over again on the doctoral project, but more than academic failure, my developing approach to ministry would fall apart.

A day or two went by with no response. Then, to my joyful amazement, one by one, folks called to say they would journey with me, including Linda. When we launched, we had about ten people who took the plunge. Since this was an academic as well as a spiritual journey, I had to set limits. It wasn't really fair, but that's the way we did it. We agreed on three months with meetings and prayer, and as the Spirit gave opportunity, we gave witness to a friend, inviting him or her to become a follower of Jesus without any regard to reward for heaven or fire insurance from hell. Many of those who took part in the group have died. On occasion, I still hear from one or two, who thank me for the experience.

Dr. Prussner liked what I did, and eventually I wrote my dissertation and was awarded the coveted Doctor of Sacred Theology from Candler School of Theology of Emory University. It had taken five years of fits and starts.

Part of the push to complete the project came when our family realized my father's prostate cancer was rapidly taking his life. I finished in the summer of 1975, and he died in October 1976. My personal and theological outlook would be forever altered. I had taken a quantum leap into the theological unknown and lived to tell the tale. The experience sent me further down the road to exciting personal and theological liberation. The contours of the liberation were anything but clear. Still, I knew that my own journey of faithing had entered a new, fresh phase.

Here I trumpet the most important single course in theology I took in four years of college, three years of seminary, and five years of graduate school. Dr. Manfred Hoffmann, a scholar from Germany, offered a course at Candler he called "The New Hermeneutic." Frankly, I did not know the "old" hermeneutic. Theological hermeneutic deals with biblical interpretation. Dr. Hoffman, drawing especially on the groundbreaking work of Rudolf Bultmann, was offering a new way to deal with Scripture. The new hermeneutic said that the interpreter, the exegete of Scripture, must be existentially involved in the text if anything of importance is to emerge. Dr. Hoffman's approach fit just right with my own developing existential sense of faith.

The seminar helped me immeasurably to fill in even more of the blanks. I had been taught to interpret the Scripture. To be sure, use good scholarly and linguistic tools to deal with Holy Writ. Dr. Hoffman did not disparage the use of tools, but he drilled into us the maxim that unless the Scripture interpreted us, we were nowhere in understanding the meaning of the text in our particular situation. He urged us not to go plunging headlong into a text until and unless we had found ourselves in the text. That is, for instance, unless the parable of the prodigal son spoke to me personally, in the depths of my being, I had no business preaching from that text next Sunday. Don't force the text. Go to something else that did communicate authentically to my own life situation at the moment. Come back later to the prodigal son when I could find my own meaning in the story as well as do my best to discern the author's intention. Hoffman's approach, through no little use of Bultmann, greatly reinforced my confidence in my own understanding of existentialism.

We used a book by the late, great Robert Funk titled *Language, Hermeneutic, and Word of God*. Funk points out that we are creatures of language, an altogether human invention. Human language, our unique evolutionary gift, and experience must interact with the biblical text if the text is to become the word of God for me. I take that assertion to mean that without the myness of human experience mixed in with the text, the words on the page remain essentially that—words on the page. Only after many years did I realize that this same Robert Funk, whom I eventually came to know briefly and most cordially, was the founder of the Jesus Seminar. The Jesus Seminar set much of contemporary New Testament scholarship on a new, controversial, and, for me, highly productive path. Out of Dr. Funk's heart, mind, and scholarship came much of the energy for the extraordinarily exciting "Jesus of history" breakthrough that I came to embrace into the depths of my being twenty-five years later. More, much more, on that adventure later. In fact, my encounter with Dr. Funk and Dr. Hoffman will form the background of what I want to describe as my own foray into personal faithing, best understood as poetry and imagination.

The Calhoun years proved quite generative for us. Not only did I finish my degree at Emory, but Linda earned her master's degree in school counseling. I was able to provide leadership to the church to relocate from a cramped main street location to a spacious lot around the corner and see the congregation build a gorgeous new sanctuary that yet stands as an architectural gem, reflecting a more open and liberating approach to worship. Sad to say, my father died during those years after an extended battle with prostate cancer. Andy, Ben, and Elizabeth flourished. Again, we made lifelong friends, many of whom we cherish to this day. All in all, the congregation and I were a nearly perfect fit.

During the Calhoun years I began to incorporate more of my theological discoveries in my preaching and teaching. The town and church were completely open to racial harmony, though we had no African-American members of the church. A historic cluster of black families had lived in Calhoun for generations and had become part of the culture. The public schools were completely integrated, fostering even more racial harmony. Still, I did not venture as far theologically as I would later. Sometimes lay people ask of their minister, "Why didn't you tell us what you had learned in seminary?" The preacher might reply, "I was afraid you would reject me and my teaching." At a level my new thinking had not matured enough for me to go too far. By the lights of some of my Calhoun parishioners, I was well ahead of the prevailing preacher culture. Still, I was cautious while maintaining a good measure of derring-do.

As I have previously mentioned, I would not come into my own theologically until the 1990s and my years at the Briggs Church. The fuller flowering came beginning in 2006 when our progressive Baptist church became part of the open-minded, welcoming, and affirming next-door Westmoreland Congregational United Church of Christ (not the fundamentalist Texas Church of Christ). I made the delightful and highly stimulating leap from ordination as a Baptist minister to that of a minister "with standing" in the United Church of Christ, by some measures the most liberal theologically and culturally of all the mainline Protestant groups in the country. To my delight I found a few dozen people in Westmoreland Church who were already ahead of me who welcomed the degree of freedom and exploration that animated me. But that's yet a later part of this journey. I did not realize it in 1979, but I was about to take some giant leaps not only with my career but in my overall thinking. I was on my way from calling myself a Christian in any traditional sense to understanding myself as a Jesus person. Just not quite yet.

When we moved to Calhoun in 1971, I quickly understood how fondly many people in the town regarded, by then, Governor Jimmy Carter, who had been elected in 1970. He preached for me two times in Vienna in the 1960s, and I saw Governor Carter briefly when he visited the Atlanta church during graduate school. Other than those snatches, I had no contact with him at all. Literally within days of our moving to Calhoun, the governor's oldest son, Jack, married Judy Langford, who had grown up in Calhoun and whose family had deep political and friendship ties with the Carters. Bert Lance, Calhoun's iconic banker who had done as much as any businessman in the region to foster the exploding carpet industry, had been appointed by the governor to head the state highway department, a key office in Georgia government. Terry Adamson, a young man then, who had grown up in the town and moved on to become a mover and shaker behind the scenes, was likewise a strong Carter supporter. And more.

Linda and I became fast friends with Jack and Judy Carter and Judy's parents, Edna and J. B. Langford. When rumors began to fly through the state that Jimmy Carter, who was limited to one term as governor, would run for president of the United States, we dismissed them as pipe dreams. Then, one day, Jack Carter came to my office to announce, "My father is indeed going to make a run for the presidency."

The formal announcement of Jimmy Carter's candidacy set the town in high gear. What had seemed political puff in the wind steadily became a political reality. I did not actively campaign, but Linda could and did, even to the point of flying with Judy Carter on one of her campaign swings through the Midwest.

The night of the election in November 1976, we waited breathlessly in the hotel suite with Jack and Judy Carter and a host of equally tense supporters. Then it was done. Jimmy Carter had been elected the thirty-ninth president of the United States. By then I had drunk a large bottle of Pepto-Bismol to settle my tossing stomach.

From friends who had Washington connections with previous presidents, I had learned that all of them since Eisenhower had someone on their staff who related to the religious community. That's the exact job I wanted with the Carter administration. I got there eventually but in a roundabout way. Our family went to the inauguration and did some of the exciting stuff that people do with such massive events. In February 1977 President and Mrs. Carter came to Calhoun to visit their family and to take part in the baby dedication of Jason, Jack and Judy's newborn son (Baptists do not do infant baptisms. Baptists do parent/child dedications). That's what brought the president to town and to our church, certainly one of the incredibly exciting times in my ministry before or since. Later, Rosalynn Carter made a solo visit to Calhoun and wound up at our house for Sunday lunch, an event that nearly put Linda in rigors for a few minutes—another story for a different time. That visit clued us in to the unfolding Labor Day Camp David meeting between the president, Anwar Sadat, and Menachem Begin and set my pulse racing even more to become part of the White House staff.

So much happened fast. I helped put together an event at the White House for National Bible Week. As part of that celebration, Linda and I spent Thanksgiving 1978 in the White House and slept in the famous Lincoln bedroom.

Along the way Jody and others from the White House staff we had come to know called with some regularity, seeking ideas for speeches by President and Mrs. Carter at family and religious occasions, which I was only too glad to supply. The big moment came when I hit upon an idea for the speech the president would give for the formal signing of the historic Israeli-Egyptian Peace Treaty. Through Reverend John Nichols and Reverend Walker Knight I picked up the phrase, "Peace, like war, is waged." I built my totally unsolicited speech around that idea and mailed it (no emails, no faxes) to Mrs. Carter's press secretary. A few hours before the great event, Jody called to alert Linda and me to get to a television because the president was using my speech. What a day!

Soon after that penultimate moment came the call for me to fly to Washington to interview for a job as a presidential speechwriter. The rest is history— that is, my history. Amidst much national press hoopla, I joined the White House staff in May 1979 for what would become a fabulous ride for Linda and me and our family. During our time on the staff, Linda, with Calhoun friend and Rosalynn Carter's fellow mother-in-law, Edna Langford, wrote *Rosalynn: Friend and First Lady*. Researching the book gave Linda some memorable hours with Mrs. Carter. After the White House days ended, I wrote about the overall experience in my book *Preacher at the White House*. With these books available I will not recap those two great years here. I will say we have been able to maintain a most cordial friendship with President and Mrs. Carter and have enjoyed important moments with them across the years, including the ceremony awarding him the Nobel Peace Prize.

Upon moving back to Plains in January 1981, President Carter began teaching Sunday school in the Maranatha Baptist Church in Plains, a practice he has continued. Across the decades, thousands of people from around the world have journeyed to the tiny village of Plains to hear the president hold forth and then have their picture made with President and Mrs. Carter. Linda and I, along with most of our family, have made fairly frequent trips to Plains to share in the president's Bible lessons. As I write this, an opportunity for further contact with the Carters is beckoning as we discuss together ways to extend his legacy through his beloved Maranatha Church. History will be most kind and appreciative of Jimmy Carter's contributions to the nation and world, both as president and then as world statesman and "wager of peace."

After President Carter lost to Ronald Reagan in 1980, our family bumped around with a sojourn in Greenville, North Carolina, and then a brief pastorate in Arlington, Texas. In 1984 I was asked to become executive director of the nationally recognized Americans United for the Separation of Church and State in Washington, DC. My time in the White House dealing with the rise of the religious right put me in a position to be named executive director. I greatly enjoyed the time and reveled in the chance to represent this honored American doctrine both in the United States and abroad.

By 1992, after eight busy years with Americans United, for a number of reasons, I was ready to get out of the spotlight and resume ministry as a pastor. Briggs Memorial Baptist Church in Bethesda, Maryland, came my way, and I accepted, though I took a significant pay cut to do so. Linda and others thought I had lost my mind, but being the troopers that they are, they went along with my decision. By the grace of God, the move has proved fortuitous, though fraught with traumas along the way. I remained pastor of the church until 2006 when we blended our Baptist congregation with the next-door neighbor Westmoreland Congregational Church of Christ and I joined that staff as minister of discipleship with senior pastor Rev. Rich Smith. When he accepted another church, I served for two years as acting senior pastor while the church sought a new senior minister.

I need to tell the Briggs Center story briefly. As I have previously mentioned, when I accepted the pastorate of Briggs Memorial Baptist Church, the membership had significantly declined. Fortunately, the church had financial reserves that enabled us to carry on a strong ministry even though our numbers were few. We quickly attracted a host of young adults through friends and family members, most of whom had mutual ties with Baylor University, where many of these newcomers had gone to school. In time these young people married, moved, got other jobs—the normal flow of today's churches. Along the way we again received a substantial bequest that extended organizational life well into the future. At the same time, the leaders of the church and I realized we were spending a significant amount of our funds on building upkeep. After considerable thought and prayer we decided to sell the building to another congregation if one should come along. In the providence of God, within a few weeks of that fateful decision, a Korean-American congregation contacted us and offered us exactly what a church real-estate firm had suggested some months previously.

It took almost two years to work our way through some quirky language in the original deed. Finally, it all came together, enabling us to sell the building, purchase a house right next door to use as headquarters for the newly invented Briggs Church, and arrange with the new congregation for us to pay rent so we could continue to use the building for worship and programs.

We had hardly settled into this new arrangement when friends from our neighbor, Westmoreland Congregational United Church of Christ, came for a visit to learn more clearly what we were doing now. The long and short is that after another prolonged time of conversation, the two congregations, ours and theirs, decided we would become one. In the course of those negotiations, the Briggs Church leadership created the Briggs Center for Faith and Action, a stand-alone nonprofit, religious but non-sectarian service organization to work in education, hunger, immigration, prison reform, hospitality, spiritual formation, and other needs as they presented themselves. I became part-time executive director as well as a member of the Westmoreland Church staff. When Tim Tutt came to Westmoreland Church as senior minister in 2012, I resigned from the church staff and became the full-time leader of the Briggs Center, a position I continue to hold at this writing. I would love to tell the entire Briggs Center story, but that's for another effort. Suffice it to say that the Briggs Center continues to move ahead. With the shift from the church staff to full time at Briggs, Linda began to take a larger role in the work of the center. Always, she had been a source of energy and imagination, but since 2012 she has served on the small staff as director of development, enabling us to cast ourselves into the future. At this writing we are more involved than ever, "sailing on the sea of faith" amidst constantly changing winds.

Thus endeth the broad outline of the journey, but not quite yet.

Excursus. In another of those fortuitous conversations with Bill Rogers, he pointed me to Martha Nussbaum's book *Upheavals of Thought.* Within the first few pages of the book, not an easy read as Bill had warned, a clue about myself jumped out. What could I learn from my emotions, even neglected, beneath-the-surface emotions? I had earlier asked myself whence the existential confidence and restless ambiguity that had framed my faithing journey even down to this day. Pulling on long-forgotten emotions, it began to dawn on me that much of my journey had been singular. I readily celebrate the various communities of love and relationship that have nurtured me. At the same time I began to isolate a series of go-it-alone times. During the years of World War II, our family moved a bewildering number of times, meaning for me as a child, a constant array of new schools. I can remember maybe a day of unease in a new school, but I must have adjusted quickly because I do not recall the terrors of newness lasting long. I attended that Vacation Bible School in the housing projects alone. I began attending the neighborhood Baptist church in Portsmouth alone. Alone, in fifth I began reading books, whole books on my own, somewhat to the dismay of my father who wanted me to play ball with my brothers. At about fourteen my mother got me my first job in the local grocery store, sacking groceries and taking the bags to customers' cars in those days before do-it-yourself technology. At sixteen I learned to be a checker, using the old clickety-clack cashier machine. I went by myself to the military boarding school in eleventh grade. As a high school senior, reflecting my love for classical music (where did that come from?), Mother gave me a season ticket to the Atlanta Symphony. I rode the bus to attend concerts in downtown Atlanta at night alone. I made the decision alone to venture to Texas for college. Family and friends always remained in my orbit. Still, I was often singular. Could this singularity have fed the confidence to take new paths? Could these emotions have enabled me to deal with multiple ambiguities without too much personal trauma?

My parents, though loving and caring, were not touchy-feely people. As far as I can recall, they never asked me "How is it going?" about anything. We were never neglected. What I thought or how I felt never came up, to my recall. As I have previously noted, my parents did not seem to look back with much reflection. They just moved on. Even as prostate cancer closed in around my sixty-seven-year-old father, I have no memory of any effort on his part to make "sense" of what was happening. Neither did he give any evidence of fear of dying or being dead. Maybe his Billy Graham revival faith from 1950 sustained him. My mother was anything but reflective about his death and dying. They loved each other and loved the four of us. But trying to sort through or put the pieces together never surfaced, to my memory. In all likelihood I inherited their measure of existential confidence, though such a phrase would never have entered their heads or come forth as words, i.e. life as full of ambiguities. Their lives, like the rest of us, had abundant ambiguities, but so far as I know, they never puzzled long over any whys.

Now, like Virginia and Bob Sr., I am moving on. Unlike them, I am puzzling through my own reflections.

In the next chapter I want to talk about the incredibly fulfilling and challenging part of this faithing journey that takes me into "poetry and imagination." Remember, this piece is not aimed to be an autobiography but a selective memoir, as it were, a poetic flight into my decades of human existence as a Christian person—more precisely, for the last twenty-five years as a Jesus person.

CHAPTER SEVEN

Faithing Toward Freedom: Theology as Poetry

Increasingly, as my theological and faithing years have moved along, I have come to surmise that poetry and imagination better get to the heart of my theology, my faithing journey, rather than heavy rhetoric and dogmatic propositions. This framework comes from several angles from a variety of readings, conferences, and sessions with theologically and poetically oriented friends.

The Bible as Poetry

It actually took me a long time to internalize that real human men and a few women, in their own real time, wrote the stories, had the visions, sang the poetry, filtered the cultural and religious messages of their times that made their way into my beloved book, the Hebrew/Christian Bible.

Another important piece of my faithing journey came when I took yet another poetic leap. I internalized that the Hebrew and Christian writings are approximations. What we have in the scriptures are distillations of the way certain groups of men and women, primarily Near Eastern folks in mundane history sought to connect with God, with the Holy, in all their myriad iterations. These spiritual ancestors wanted to get inside their own feelings about this penultimate relationship. Such moments are always reduced to art, to words as they get passed along, yet mere words cannot encapsulate such grand, soaring, even frightful experiences—hence, metaphor and poetry. Theology is not 2 + 2. Theology grows out of a person's deep longings to know and be known by what the person regards as Holy, Other.

How did the Hebrew and Christian canons (lists) come into being?

First, the Hebrew Bible. After a series of tragically unsuccessful, murderous Jewish wars (c. 66–136 CE) with Roman occupying armies, groups of religious Jewish leaders gradually reached the decision to create a canon, a list of sacred writings the Jews could use with confidence in worship. This decision became crucial when the Roman armies utterly destroyed the magnificent Herodian Jerusalem Jewish temple in the early 70s CE. From antiquity the Jerusalem temple, destroyed and rebuilt at least once (see Nehemiah and Ezra), had stood at the center of Jewish religious life. With the center gone, as it turned out for good, Jewish religious leaders gravitated to the voluminous writings Jews regarded as sacred. With apologies for this shorthand version, the Jews thus became people of the book. With the temple gone, orders of priests who tended to celebrate temple worship were replaced by teachers, scholars, and rabbis (hence the term "rabbinical Judaism").

In the course of time, these Jewish leaders also reached the decision to close the canon. No more books would be added to their sacred list. Some of their cherished writings reached back a thousand or more years. Others, such as the book of Daniel, dated from about 175 BCE. Thus, what became the Hebrew Bible, the Christian Old Testament, evolved over at least a thousand years.

This *ad hoc* band of Jewish religious leaders faced a daunting task. These gatherings of Jewish religious leaders struggled for years over which writings would be included in the list and which would be excluded. The teachers and rabbis confronted extremely difficult decisions because various clusters of Jewish believers cherished different writings. Any exclusion pained, even offended segments of the larger Jewish community scattered throughout the Roman Empire. Among some Jewish groups in our own time, the debate over the canon continues. A collection of the excluded books did meld into a significant body of writings commonly called the Apocrypha. Many Christian Bibles and faith traditions include the Apocrypha.

The Christian New Testament likewise experienced a similar but much more abbreviated evolution, about a hundred years. From the crucifixion of Jesus in approximately 30 CE, the body of writings that became the Christian New Testament evolved at least until the early decades of the second Christian century CE. Even then, it took decades beyond the actual writings about and around the story of Jesus for councils of men, by then largely Catholic bishops, to decide which books of the many in use by various Jesus groups would make it into the canon and which would be excluded. As with the Jewish writings, dozens, scores of other writings used by various clusters of Jesus people, did not make it into the authorized canon.

Again, remember that men, human men, made these difficult decisions. The various Christian leaders and councils operated within a plethora of headwinds: theological, historical, political, and ecclesiastical. As Christianity morphed into the official religion of the Roman Empire, canonical councils had to accede to imperial demands regarding politically sensitive issues.

Along the way, after decades of wrangling, the books that made the list generated sufficient votes from the members of the councils to get included in the final cut. Both the Jewish and Christian canonical decisions were made by men, creatures of their times—some gifted and deeply spiritual; others crassly political, driven by their own parochial desires.

Another *excursus*: The Jesus movement that became local churches that became Christianity had ties to evolving rabbinic Judaism.

Against incredible cultural, political, and religious odds, the Jesus movement kept alive and mythologized the life, death, and resurrection of Jesus. Over decades this movement morphed into churches. Able and not-so-able leaders of local and regional congregations morphed into parish priests and into bishops governing clusters of congregations. It (just *it*) was gradually decided that these followers of Jesus and Paul needed their own Holy Writ bearing the stamp of approval of church fathers or councils, a moving target in those early decades of the Jesus movement. In short, if the Jews from which the Jesus movement came to life had their book, the Christians likewise needed their book. Another push for creation of the Christian canon probably also came when it seemed Jesus was not soon returning.

Compilations of Holy Writ existed among even more ancient faiths, such as Hinduism, Buddhism, and others. When Islam emerged in the fifth century CE, Muslims developed their own book, the Koran. Since we humans learned to write down what we say and think eons ago, uncounted editions of Holy Writ have happened, with most groups declaring that only their books were truly from God or the gods and theirs alone worth following. *Finis the excursus.*

Concurrently with these historical developments within the faiths, learned, powerful Jewish rabbis and a host of Christian leaders along the way began to posit that ordinary flesh-and-blood human beings, authors of the selected writings, were possessed of splendid insights into matters spiritual. Going a step further, these religious leaders decided the authors of the "books" wrote under a measure of grand imbuement from God; they wrote with "divine inspiration." For my part I now translate "divine inspiration" to read "spiritually infused poetry and imagination." Some did claim they wrote under unique leadership from God. But I have the idea that many of those ancients would be surprised to see what has happened to their efforts. At any rate, they were people like you and me with pen and paper writing down ideas and visions adorned with flights of poetry and imagination. What they wrote flowed from their own beings in terms of their own culture, and spiritually fired yearnings. What they penned often dramatically challenged their prevailing cultural norms.

In our time large bodies of Christian organizations insist the Hebrew and Christian texts come directly from God without error—inerrant truth that cannot be questioned. This line of reasoning forces the Holy Writ into tight boxes. Religious leaders who go this way are prone to tolerate no deviation from the text—that is, as the way they read the text. Unfortunate mistreatment of the power and drama of the texts often occurs. Bumper-sticker religion emerges: *The Bible says it; I believe it; that settles it!* Sad to say, these folks rarely ask what "it" is they want to accept without question.

As the Jewish and Christian faiths unfolded over the common era, other men (and maybe a few women) wrote what has come to us as theology, dogma, doctrine. How do we get dogma, doctrine? Follow me along this trail for bit. Marcus Borg, in his books, lectures, and recordings, introduced me to a helpful flow. In various ways, Dr. Borg concludes that we humans tend to go from experience to metaphor to doctrine. Translated, this means to me that along the way, we have a powerful, life-changing experience. The experience can be personal, historical, political, religious, whatever. You name it. In the realm of the spiritual, we experience a moment we regard as a breakthrough from God to us. Our lives take on new directions because of the experience. We rarely keep these epiphanies secret. We want to tell someone of the epiphenomenal moment. How do we do this? We use metaphor. We say, "It was like…a song came to me…the heavens opened…a voice came out of the dark…the configuration of the clouds told me…the intestines of a chicken predicted…." A metaphor, like poetry, points beyond itself as a way to get inside, describe a moment beyond itself.

Not content with the spoken or sung metaphor, either we ourselves or a friend or a wise sage comes to the conclusion that the world needs to know about the experience. She sets about to write it down on clay tablets or papyrus or vellum or paper, to freeze-frame the moment, to elide the experience from metaphor to dogma. The next thing we know, someone is saying this experience is *a* way. Then, *the* way God speaks to all now and for all time. For us humans, creatures of language, especially language written in ink on paper, if we are not careful, the printed word becomes an end itself. The glorious experience, special to you then, under the aegis of religious shamans, becomes normative, doctrine for all people henceforth. At least that's the way the vision plays out in mundane (Cantwell Smith) history.

For instance, I readily agree that Paul of Acts had an experience on the road to Damascus or some existential breakthrough drama. By his several reports in his letters to new, struggling clusters of Jesus people, that experience radically changed his life. Paul and others trying to get inside the experience used poetic metaphors of "heavenly light" and "voices," common ingredients as people across the centuries rhapsodized their revelatory experiences. From his Damascus road experience Paul and others who had similar moments declared that in those epiphenomenal events, Jesus, the crucified, risen Christ of God, broke through to them. They had met none other than the exalted Christ, raised by God to a new, beyond-this-life existence. Their earnest, well-meaning testimonies became paving stones on our forebears' road, leading to the metamorphosis that changed Jesus of Nazareth to Jesus the Christ.

These people, mainly men, from their experiences or reports from others with stature like Paul, then developed what became early Christianity. The evolution had anything but a steady, neatly unfolding trajectory. To the contrary the unfolding had ups and downs, zigs and zags, frequently generating huge verbal and, sad to say, all-too-often armed conflicts. Even the most untutored observer can ascertain that early Christianity was anything but settled. In fact, in the twenty-first century neither Christianity nor any other such grand movement remains static. Great movements, including religions, change or die.[9] For me, underlying confidence in the grace of God and faithing with no boundaries energize rather than diminish my days lived in the milieu of these ongoing delightful ambiguities. (Do not put a period where God has put a comma.)

Paul soon felt persuaded by this vision to trek through vast regions of the Near Eastern Roman world (Asia Minor). He proclaimed that the crucified Galilean Jew Jesus, whom he declared he had met on the road, was indeed God's messiah sent to save the world from sin. Jesus groups scattered in some of the cities of the Roman Empire grew out of Paul's words and ministry, abetted in ways we can only imagine by other trekking Jesus missionaries.

Paul wrote over a period of maybe twenty years (c. 40–60 CE), well before the canonical Gospels (Matthew, Mark, Luke, and John) came into being.

In those years he developed a theology (doctrine, dogma) of Jesus as Christ, Messiah, a Christology. Where did he get his Christology? I have a hunch (only a hunch but still fairly well-informed). Scattered Jesus cell groups either had persisted from Jesus' own ministry in Galilee and/or formed around his legacy after the crucifixion. The canonical Gospels and the book of Acts offer tantalizing tidbits that point retrospectively toward some residual effect of Jesus' time among them. Clearly the death of Jesus did not mean the death of the movement. The book of Acts and some of Paul's letters indicate that James, Jesus' brother, generated an echo in Jerusalem of Jesus' life, ministry, and death. We ache to know more about the Jesus movement in those years immediately after the cross.

As I try to wrap my mind around the early Paul, so crucial to the development of the Jesus movement, I conjecture he extrapolated his theology first from his own negative encounters with these Jesus cell groups in and around Jerusalem. From his own testimony Paul did not like these groups, whatever their persona, and sought to stamp them out as heretics. Everything changed for Paul when he had his vision on the Damascus road. From there he began some process of developing his theology of and about Jesus. He insists God gave him his theology directly (Gal 1:12); that's probably a stretch. He would have had some conversations with those first- or second-generation followers of Jesus. He folded in predictive snatches from Hebrew texts he would have known quite well. How and why he drew such dramatic conclusions remains a matter of ongoing speculation down to our present time. Important work on Paul continues steadily, inviting productive reading and contemplation. What I have imagined is anything but definitive, but it gives me a place from which to dig into more Pauline studies. And why Jesus? Godly, smart, compassionate men likewise bucked the prevailing religious system and died at the hands of the Romans, often on crosses. Why then Jesus? Why this man who had been crucified by the Romans as seditious? Why this man who had fostered cell groups that infuriated Paul? Other revolutionaries who challenged the system and died for their efforts likewise left behind cell groups. Devoted followers of John the Baptist, who lost his head (Mark 6:21–29), persisted as groups for decades into the Christian era. Did Paul's antagonistic exposure to the Jesus cell groups flip to positive affirmation? Probably many theological doctoral dissertations aimed to penetrate that mystery gather dust on scholars' shelves.

As Paul walked the Roman Empire he established those urban cell groups through which he aimed to teach Jesus as he understood Jesus. As far as we know as previously noted Paul gave only snatches of biographical information about Jesus: "Born of a women," (Galatians 4:4) and the Lord's Supper narratives (1 Corinthians 11:27-36). With soaring poetic language Paul preached Jesus, whom he now proclaimed as the Christ, crucified to redeem the world from sin. In equally majestic words he sang of Jesus raised by the power of God (1 Corinthians 15:3-9) but no Easter Sunday morning stories.

Paul's paeans of praise for Jesus demonstrate my point about theology as poetry. Messiah, incarnate Son of God, redeemer of the world, raised by the power of God, heaven—all are faith statements, affirmations of Paul's deepest devotion to his personal image of Jesus, whom he evidently never saw in the flesh. He lifted heart and song (see Phil 2:5–11) to celebrate the spiritual unphotographable experience that captured him on the Damascus road. None of these classic epithets can be quantified, nor did Paul intend to quantify them. In his own way he was singing about his experience with the vision he declared came from Jesus.

As he traveled and established Jesus cell groups, he obviously began to pen his celebration of the life-changing moment—from experience to metaphor to doctrine. In numerous Roman Empire cities he spent time with diaspora Jews and receptive non-Jews, telling them about his experience and explaining the vision as a heavenly visitation by the risen Jesus. Moving on to the next preaching point, he wrote letters back to the groups he had recently evangelized into the ways of Jesus now as Christ. A new expression of faith so tender struggling to gain traction in the religiously glutted empire would have generated many questions and disputes, especially after Paul left one place to journey to another city where he would plant or encourage yet another Jesus group. To help shore up the shaky faith of his Jesus groups, he wrote letters.

From numerous sources another aspect of Paul's traveling ministry has captured my attention of late: his theology, his Christology, as a work in progress. As I have noted, after Jesus' death, groups memorializing his life and ministry sprang up in and around Jerusalem. In the longer sweep of history, these remnants became seeds from which grew the Christian church. The Judean cell groups possibility notwithstanding, the Jesus movement in the larger Roman world in all likelihood did not exist before Paul. In his surviving letters he maintained the basics of the risen Christ as God's savior while steadi-ly adjusting his ideas to fit specific crises and opportunities in his churches: meat offered to idols, meaning of the Lord's Supper, speaking in tongues, etc. Questions and disputes in one Jesus cluster prompted Paul to think further about the meaning of the vision and to elaborate or explain to the questioning group. His, then, was a theological, christological work in progress written as he and small bands of helpers trudged the roads of the empire. To perceive his theology neatly formed is to miss the dynamism of his pioneering work.

Of the many epistles he probably wrote, only a few gained purchase among the aborning Jesus movement's cell groups. Others are lost or withered away from inattention. First- and second-century church fathers, over decades of debate, decided which of Paul's extant letters would have their blessing to become part of the canon used by the Jesus groups, now churches. What's more, these fathers decided the letters they affirmed worthy of the canon were uniquely inspired of God. In time these letters and other documents that were gradually voted into the canon would determine much of the content of Chris-tianity for all time. Thus again, the Borg flow: from experience (Damascus road) to metaphor (light and voices) to doctrine extrapolated from the letters to the churches Paul wrote. Add in other books voted into the canon by the bishops, and we have the twenty-seven books of the New Testament, eventu-ally regarded by many as the inerrant word of God. For seventeen or eighteen centuries these writings have shaped official doctrines for Christianity.

From my vantage point in the twenty-first century, as the years roll by, I remain amazed at how much ink and paper we have collectively expended across the centuries debating fine points of those letters and other canonical writings. What gives arcane laws and rituals from such Hebrew Bible books as Leviticus—compiled by unknown writers more than 3,000 years ago in another time and culture—power over faith and practice in our day? Why has traditional Christianity established Paul's lyrical, experiential theology written on the run from 2,000 years ago the final authority over Christian faith and practice in this century? True, the basic human needs for health, hope, peace, community, and connection with the Ultimate remain. The specifics between Paul's world and ours have changed dramatically and continue to evolve inexorably. The role of women, children, sexual orientation, government, economics, technology make our world different from his calling us to an ever-unfolding of faith and relationship with the Ultimate in the twenty-first century. What's more, contemporary study of the developing Jesus groups readily reveals serious disconnects from one group to the next. If Paul could not settle faith issues in his own day by personal ministry and his letters, what makes us think we can come to lockstep agreement using his letters as binding rules 2,000 years down the pike? The fact that a faith-perspective labeled Christian exists today in myriad expressions calls into serious question any assertion of inerrancy. Lest we think disparagingly of Paul's peripatetic theological method, let's confess that like Paul of old we are still making up our approaches to faith on the run. For many of us, our faithing journey is never settled, the final destination never reached, the final form impossible. That's the joy and hazard of faith fraught with ambiguities with no boundaries. We live with a faith perspective that says we will never go beyond God despite our evolving attempts to understand God. The ambiguities offer golden opportunities to think and rethink our relationship with the Ultimate.

What's more, as my own journey has unfolded, I increasingly ask what makes Paul's letters normative while thousands of other similar letters written by equally convinced followers of Jesus did not make it into the canon? The Didache, Gospel of Thomas, Gospel of Mary, Gospel of Peter, various Gnostic writings, on and on the list unfolds of equally ancient writings that did not make the cut. What guided the fathers to pick and choose among the extant writings of Paul? What were their own theological bents that pushed them in their selections? And why were books with questionable Pauline authorship included? A host of Pauline scholars are all but sure that such books, for instance 1 and 2 Timothy, with more restrictive views of women and church discipline in general, were almost certainly not written by Paul. Gorgeous writings like Ephesians and Colossians raise serious questions about Pauline authorship. It could well be these letters were penned by later Jesus people in the apostle's name, a common practice in those pre-copyright days. Maybe the deciding fathers were not aware of questions about authorship. Or maybe these books that raised Pauline questions fit the prevailing attitudes among the leaders of the expanding Jesus movement.

At the risk of sounding flip, as I have said before, these letters and the other parts of the Christian canon had the votes of the church fathers in various councils to make their way into the New Testament. Growing usage among the spreading Jesus groups, churches, encouraged the emerging ecclesiastical rulers—"bishops," they called themselves, echoing the title of local Roman governors—to vote for the letters and accounts we now have. It's also informative to remember that profound political and Roman imperial issues often shaped the bishops' decisions as church and empire merged. If the sitting emperor in the third and fourth centuries CE leaned toward a certain theological/political point of view, the bishops who ruled at his pleasure found it difficult to go against His Imperial Majesty.

I readily declare most of the writings in the New Testament, like many pieces of the Hebrew Bible, are sublime, gorgeous, powerful, full of meaningful insight into the long human journey to find faith and footing in a world often tossed and torn. Inspired uniquely by God, worthy of unquestioned acceptance, normative for Christian faith for all time, bulwarks against hell, and manuals for making it to heaven, worth all the effort expended to parse them out across the centuries strikes me as a monumental, historic stretch. For my part I do not have a wholesale replacement for either the Hebrew Bible or the Christian New Testament. I find in many of these texts more than enough encouragement, enlightenment, and common sense to last well beyond my lifetime. At the same time I have no problem seeing much of Holy Writ and theology generated across the centuries as grand, even noble human attempts to find and reinforce faith. In short, I understand these efforts as products of flights of gorgeous poetry, energized spiritual imagination, cumulative tradition.

I am a grateful product of eons of cumulative tradition. I thank God and my genetic ancestors for their legacy to me, resulting in my measure of existential confidence laced through with ambiguity. Here also, the confidence in the grace of God enables me to embrace and pursue new directions, trying always to fill in more blanks of what I do not know, even what I don't know that I don't know. I can joyfully, yet humbly liberate myself from a literalistic ball-and-chain attachment to the Hebrew Bible and the Christian New Testament. In the same moment I tell one and all I am a Christian, a Jesus person, a follower in the Way , a Bible person with bountiful hope yet with no illusions. As a Christian, remember, I cherish the Bible and take it seriously, just not always literally.

Cumulative Tradition: Peeling Faithing's Onion

Let's take a breath and fold in a bit more fully Cantwell Smith's concept of cumulative tradition. Recall Smith was Harvard professor of comparative history of religion and the author of *The Meaning and End of Religion.* As a scholar on world religions, he used the concept of cumulative tradition to understand how all the world's great religions began and continue to evolve (as do nations, families, sports lore, etc.). For me, as a Christian, I paid special attention as he discussed the way the Christian approaches to faith are shaped from and by unfolding, evolving cumulative tradition.

Cumulative points toward accumulation. Tradition points to ideas, motifs, practices that have a definable (mundane), observable history. Cumulative tradition then points to the layering of traditions in detectable, traceable history. Beliefs and personal faith cannot be measured empirically. Smith says, "Cumulative tradition means the entire mass of overt objective data that constitute the historical deposit of the past religious life of the community in question (Christian, Jewish, Muslim, Hindu, Buddhist, etc.)." He says "temples, scriptures, theological systems, dance patterns, legal and other social institutions, conventions, moral codes, myths and, etc., anything that can be and is transmitted from one person, one generation to another, and that a historian can observe" are the stuff of cumulative traditions that shape one's personal and collective worldview.[10]

The living out in daily life of these beliefs and faith expressions can be seen and measured. We humans build these traditions that frame our lives, making us better or worse. Every human who has lived on the earth builds their own tradition, consciously or unconsciously, on purpose and/or on mental and spiritual autopilot. I am a product of a long and winding tradition, reaching back into my own infinity. I am also hourly, daily involved in adding to/building more of that tradition that I pass on to my family and friends. As Americans we are the products of a tradition, good and not so good. As people who call themselves Christians, we are part of/products of a multilayered tradition, reaching back to Jesus and beyond.

Recently, a star athlete was accused of beating his child. When a national cry went up about his behavior, he called his treatment "discipline." Besides, he said, this is the way his parents reared him. Heavy corporal punishment had become entrenched as a destructive tradition in his life and then in child rearing. Was he simply a hapless, powerless victim of his tradition? Was he simply passing on his own cumulative tradition to his children? Though mightily shaped by our tradition, we are not powerless to change bad traditions in our own time. As I have noted, strains of Islam seem to say that if one dies a martyr for Allah, taking innocent victims with him, he or she is immediately transported to a glorious heaven full of all manner of charms and rewards. Does such a destructive religious tradition provide impetus for the murderous terrorism that plagues our time?

As I write, the nation is in another round of confronting white supremacy, super-nationalism, framed, sadly, by ever-present neo-Nazism. Folks, largely white men, who buy into this ethos are the products of cumulative tradition that persuades them that only white people—make that white men—are worthy to lead and control the country. If these men took the time, they could dissect their own feelings, trace their impulses to in-life (mundane) events that pushed them in this tragic, destructive direction.

We are presently laboring under a president's leadership who likewise could trace his attitudes to those passed on to him by his father and grandfather. He, like the rest of us, is a product of cumulative tradition. He, like us, is not irrevocably bound by that tradition. We can change, learn from, break out of our formative traditions, with effort and thought. Unfortunately, most of us do not choose to exercise the effort to move beyond the forces of cumulative tradition.

The contours of traditions in and of one era may become more or less indistinct with the passage of time. However, given the retentive power both of our human brain and the binding power of a specific cultural configuration, traditions never fully go away. Cumulative tradition, unexamined, can take on the cast of immutable, irrefutable, unexamined fact (i.e., white supremacy, inerrant Scripture). Stories abound of family feuds carried from one generation to the next. In time a third- or fourth-generation feuder does not really know what the fight is about, only that the feud continues inexorably, shaping every aspect of the family's relationships.

Remember, people create traditions that build and build in history. Traditions can and should be studied and measured. Traditions can be resolutely held and yet be monumentally wrong.

I am a southerner born in 1937 in Atlanta, Georgia. I actually know little of my ancestral history beyond three grandparents and a few uncles, aunts, and cousins whom I knew in the flesh. But I am a product of unknown forebears going all the way back. Why do I like broiled calf liver and onions when my children gag at the very idea of such a meal? If I wanted to, I could probably trace my enjoyment of such a repast to some long-forgotten relatives. Since traditions accumulate in mundane history, they can become known. Now, in the twenty-first century, mix in the science of DNA and genetics, and our traditions take on an even deeper shaping significance. I can hear Tevye singing, "Tradition! Tradition!" in *Fiddler on the Roof.*

What has cumulative tradition to do with religion, specifically the Christian religion and more particularly my own expression of the Christian religion now at eighty as poetry? And how can I find a new sense of liberation as I employ Cantwell Smith's rubric? What does it mean when I declare I choose to frame my faithing at eighty in terms of the cumulative Christian tradition handed down to me layer upon layer from countless Christian ancestors? And more to the point, I may steadily move beyond many of the traditions that have accumulated, framing the Christian religion from centuries past, and still emphatically, joyfully locate myself as a Christian, a Jesus person.

My earliest Christian ancestors with whom I genetically and culturally connect, in their time and milieu, used the mental and cultural tools they had. They appropriated aspects of the developing Jesus story that made sense to them at the time. Epiphenomenal breakthroughs happened all the time they were told. People, especially noted kings and warriors, sometimes came back from the dead, they were told.

Though those first-century folks never actually saw anyone come back from the dead, they chose to accept these stories (traditions) as bits of history, namely Julius Caesar and Emperor Nero back from the dead. From earlier antiquity Egyptian pharaohs reportedly (traditions) had glorious lives in the afterlife. That centuries-long Egyptian tradition led to the building of giant pyramids and other fantastically elaborate and expensive tombs.

A case in point: in the earliest development of the Jesus tradition, word got out that the movement hero, Jesus' friend and disciple, Peter, had actually seen the empty tomb as reported in Luke's Gospel (about 80 CE and John about 90 CE). Later, reports of a book written probably between 150 and

200 CE called "The Gospel of Peter" began to attract attention, not all of it positive, by church fathers (notice, reports of such a book). As with all of the New Testament documents, no original copy has been found. A fragment of the Gospel of Peter dating from the eighth or ninth century CE was found in Egypt in 1886. The author of the book—not Simon Peter, who was long dead—wrote that Peter had seen the towering angels and the risen Christ come out of the tomb. The figure the writer describes glowed and flowed. As it emerged from the grave, the figure stretched from earth to heaven. Apparently, early followers of Jesus jumped at the chance likewise to believe in the empty tomb narrative. It apparently did not discombobulate those early Jesus people when Peter's "account" portrayed a Jesus figure emerging from the tomb reaching to the sky. It is also important to note that many church fathers rejected the book as not meeting muster to make it into the canon. Adoration. Flowing language and imagery. Hence, poetry and imagination.

Fact of history or leap of faith, metaphor, poetry, sacred myth? The developing cumulative tradition of the empty tomb narrative had a galvanizing effect on those early followers who, by the middle of that first Christian century, were largely non-Jews. It is important to note the Jesus movement, now, early first century CE, almost exclusively in the Roman world, may well have withered and died without the empty tomb tradition as the Jesus movement broke the geographical bounds of Judea. Could it be the case that non-Jews needed an element of the Jesus story like the savior who broke open his grave, a narrative more closely synced with their mythologies of the gods visiting among mortals? Could it be the cumulative tradition of the virgin birth, not mentioned by Mark, John, or Paul, likewise fit the ethos of the non-Jewish Roman world as the Jesus movement took hold in the non-Jewish Roman world?

With what degree of uncritical acceptance did subsequent generations of Jesus people ascribe to the empty tomb story, to a virgin-born Jesus, to a man who could walk on water and still storms? Did these ancestors see the resurrection narrative as history or products of poetry, hope, yearning, imagination? For the most part my hunch is that they, with hardly a backward glance, took the Gospel stories as history as they understood history, as history was commonly understood in the Greco/Roman world.

Time marched on with the Christian expression of religious faith developing layer upon layer of cumulative tradition. From simple Galilean tradesmen and fishermen the movement became layered over with the elaborate trappings and theology of what became the Roman Catholic Church. Then along comes the lifting of the intellectual veils with the European Enlightenment beginning in the late seventeenth century. Among many compelling if unnerving probes, scholars began seriously to examine the biblical narratives, using evolving literary, textual, linguistic, and history-of-language tools. In time the unheard of began to emerge. Jesus was not born of a virgin. He may not have been born in Bethlehem. No, he did not walk on water, still storms, and feed 5,000 with a boy's lunch. He was crucified, but he stayed dead. If these classic stories lose their historical footing, what's to happen to our Jesus faith today? We can defensively take a deep breath, impugn all that scholarship, and insist on the total, unquestioned historicity of the entire New Testament.

For my part I can revel in the richness of the ever-unfolding cumulative tradition. I can unequivocally call myself a full-fledged, card-carrying Christian in my time while regarding most of those narratives as poetry, embellished and enriched by the vivid imagination of people who wanted to follow in the Jesus way. I can celebrate the biblical songs full of hope and life and justice yet not be bound by the specifics of the ethos of the first century CE. I can readily and productively address critical human problems in my own time, using the broad themes of these ancient stories and writings, without being tethered to the worldview that produced the stories and writings. At last, then I begin to answer my freshman puzzle: what does the resurrection of Jesus have to do with my faith today? Everything existentially, just not much historically. I can be and am a Jesus person in the twenty-first century, though no longer personally, theologically dependent on the historicity of the stories and theology that shaped the opening centuries of the way of life millions of us call Christian. In short, I am deeply grateful for the traditions of which I am the beneficiary while finding the existential confidence to see many of the narratives framing the Christian past as poetry. To be sure, I find real, datable, mundane history in our collective cumulative tradition as Christians. The narratives and the theology they forge take flight across the centuries as poetry.

Twentieth-century theology, anthropology, and hermeneutic provide a working framework for me as I parse my faithing at eighty in the twenty-first century. Without attempting a history of the last century or so of theology and New Testament scholarship, certainly beyond my paygrade, I will hit a few high points of more contemporary biblical scholarship that speak to me. German theologian and New Testament scholar Rudolf Bultmann (1884–1976), drawing from many sources, framed an existential approach to the Bible, especially the Jesus narratives. In ground-shaking scholarship he proposed "demythologizing" the narratives: virgin birth, empty tomb, etc. By this Bultmann meant stripping away the aspects of these narratives that created intellectual and religious stumbling blocks to twentieth-century people seeking a faith that made sense in light of huge scientific and scholarly advances. Bultmann eventually went so far as to insist that nothing could really be known of the life of Jesus other than he was born and ultimately crucified. He did insist that God had done something dramatic and sacrificial (hence, poetic) in Jesus that offered humans who encountered God in Jesus a word of God.

The conservative Christian world rejected this notion. These folk said, "Take away the literal, datable, observable foundations of these narratives, and the Christian faith collapses as an empty fraud."

Gerd Lüdemann, a German radical contemporary New Testament scholar in his book *The Resurrection of Christ: A Historical Inquiry*, says as much. He goes through an exhaustive historical and linguistic analysis of the New Testament documents related to the resurrection and makes two primary conclusions: Twenty-first-century Christians can only have an existential experience with the visions of such founders as Peter and Paul because nothing of history exists otherwise in the accounts. He then takes a huge leap—given that the resurrection of Jesus is the central pillar of Christianity, given that the resurrection is not historical, even fabricated to dupe gullible followers of the crucified Jesus, the Christian religion is built on fraud and hence of no value; it's all over.

I do not take Lüdemann's leap. Neither do I put historical credence in the Gospel accounts of the resurrection nor other epiphenomenal New Testament narratives. Where does that leave me in my time, in my faith journey at eighty? I combine Carl Jung, Rudolf Bultmann, David Eagleman, Cantwell Smith, Marcus Borg, Gordon Cosby, Linda Maddox, Tim Tutt, and Bill Rogers, to name a few, who put me in a comfortably ambiguous, albeit restless place in my faith journey at eighty: theology as poetry.

When I look back on my ancestors and also look around today, the Jesus story, the Christian story, does not stop with the empty tomb. Those faithful few who, in time, became many kept building the Christian story/tradition layer upon cumulative layer. To them the importance of mundane history receded. Embrace of the poetry, the mystery, the hope, and promise of Easter became all the more important: Remember, "It may not have happened just like that, but it's true anyway."

Fast-forward into the decades following whatever it was that happened to Jesus' body, to Pilate, temple prelates, and the cross. Mundane history becomes less important. In our time Diana Butler Bass has done us moderns a great favor with her fertile book *A People's History of Christianity*. Bass takes us into the everyday life of Jesus' followers as the decades and centuries rolled by. Our Christian ancestors, people of the pews, largely moved beyond fights over particulars of doctrine, leaving such debates to the priests and bishops. Rather our third-, fourth-, fifth-century ancestors set about to practice the way of Jesus they could understand. They became neighbors to folks who totally disagreed with their approach to faith. When plagues struck, these Jesus people tended to the sick, balancing their own fear of dying with the hope of heaven if they succumbed to the ravages of the disease. They established crude hospitals. They provided their own version of social safety nets. From time to time, the more bold among them actually challenged the greed and arrogance of Roman Catholic prelates. While far too many of the church fathers got caught up in petty political parsing, the people sought to serve God and neighbor as they imagined Jesus acted and called them to do. The theologians may have tried to count the number of angels on a pinhead. The rank and file went on with their lives, serving one another to a commendable degree. The narratives, dramatized by elaborate pageants and parades, undoubtedly shaped their lives. But they did not spend much, if any time puzzling over the historicity of the narratives. The cumulative traditions they built on a daily basis, village by village, family by family, carried them forward becoming warp and woof their practical faithing.

So we come to the twenty-first century. With some discomfort I move away from the narratives as history. I affirm it takes a man and a woman to produce a child. Human beings do not walk on water. And once we are dead, certifiably dead, we do not come back to life. What to do with the stories historically foundational to the faith? I embrace life today, moving in the flow of the cumulative tradition. I see and sense layer upon layer of the tradition. Even a cursory study of the cumulative tradition reveals some wonderfully commendable layers, while others are littered with bigotry, intolerance, jealousy, and more. I experience generous compassion and hard-hearted fundamentalism. In joy and pain I say all this is part of the tradition of which I am part, product, and preserver.

So Poetry

My distillations of the poetic genre from several sources say that poetry is a literary form that in a wide variety of ways enables one to find or see meaning from the ordinary pieces of life, to take the second and third look at what appears before our eyes. Poetry can take us to the beyond at the most unexpected moments in our lives. Theology as poetry can have this transforming effect on us if we will allow ourselves the luxury and the angst of being transmitted on a magic carpet of the Godward flings of people who have similarly been flung Godward.

Poetry is not devoid of history. Poetry does not deny its own measure of reality. Behind a poem exists almost invariably a bit of history, some measure of discernible concreteness or commonly agreed upon fact, the mundane. A poem about a tree in springtime presupposes a tree. The poem about the tree in winter can go in a thousand different directions: how stark the bare tree loomed; the poet's memory of a barren tree on his grandfather's farm; now both the beloved or hated grandfather gone, along with the farm; the barren tree could point the poet toward the promise of spring and full leaf again. Behind a poem extolling the wonders and mysteries of human love are humans.

So my faithing journey at eighty takes me into poetry and imagination. Poets and poetry take us where ordinary (what's ordinary?) language can't manage. A newborn baby can be described in terms of height, weight, skin tone, bone, and blood (mundane history). And all that is certainly a way to describe a newborn human being. If that baby, however, is the first child of a couple who have longed for a child for years with no success hitherto, those parents will become ecstatic about that delightful bundle of joy. They may not put pen to paper and write a sonnet about their child, but their souls will soar and words become jumbled when describing the baby to colleagues gathered around the office coffee pot. You get the drift, I hope.

For twenty years or so, Linda and I and a coterie of friends and kin made the annual trek to the west front lawn of the U.S. Capitol for the grand July 4th celebration. Thousands of Americans and others from around the world pour into that majestic sweep for picnics, frolic, great music, and then the exciting fireworks that light up the National Mall. Invariably, tears of pride and joy start in my eyes when we the people rise for the "Star-Spangled Banner" and "God Bless America." Standing beneath the soaring dome of the Capitol, topped by the Statue of Freedom, I feel Lincoln's "mystic chords" that bring us together. I can lament the often tacky shenanigans under the guise of government that take place in those marbled halls. I can recognize the many political, social, religious, racial, and economic crosscurrents that run through that huge crowd. At the same time I get choked up when I go beyond the parts to reach out to the whole. I move from the crowd count to the wonder of the love of country that brings this many people to this place at this moment. That's poetry. Music and flags and soaring metaphors and fried chicken and iced tea come nearer to embracing the moment than the analyzing of the professor of political science.

Theology as poetry. I certainly did not invent the idea. I am at a loss to recall when I first ran across the notion. Maybe Cantwell Smith?[11] Dom Crossan? Marcus Borg? But I realized then and feel even more strongly today that the best way for me to deal with much of theology—doctrines that seek to determine beliefs that shape life, along with vast portions of Scripture—is to approach these entities not as rigid religious straitjackets, not as eternal truths. Rather, I have come to see the bulk of what I call theology as poetry.

When I decided to research the idea, I found considerable backing. From Wikipedia (don't scoff) comes a site by Michael N. Thomson, a book editor, who tries to get inside Christian dogma by seeing theology as poetry. In his blog from February 2011, Thomas has a fetching invitation: Whatever your theological journey or wherever on the continuum you place yourself, "leave the window ajar at dawn." That beautiful poetic metaphor certainly works for me. For a long time, especially as the years have rolled by at light speed, I have "left the window ajar at dawn." Cherish the thought; value the notion; the bottom of the page is never the end of the story; there's always more just around the bend. The minute you nail "it" down, you have closed off a refreshing, invigorating, demanding, if unsettling future.

The Bible is full of varieties of poetry: Psalms 1 and 23, Isaiah 6, Song of Deborah, Song of Solomon, Matthew 1, Luke 2, the *Magnificat* of Mary, John 1, Philippians 2, 1 Corinthians 13 and 15, all of Revelation, and much more. We miss the point when we try to take these pieces literally. Get into these passages. Find yourself in them. Go into these hallowed halls "with the window ajar at dawn." You are engaging some of the greatest literature for all time in any culture. It is as obscene to abuse these passages with literalism as it is to squeeze great poetry of any ilk into a literal straitjacket. Certainly apply language, history, commentary. And then ask the existential questions: So what? What is the transcendent word for me from these lines today? What is the universal embrace of these words?

What about biblical stories? Narrative? Adam and Eve, Noah, Abraham, Moses, etc. Realize many of these began as drama, saga, stories, songs, chants told and retold around the campfires and cooking pots of ancient, preliterate people. Those stories had poetic rhythm and meter. The origins are fascinating to contemplate.

Can none of them be taken as history, especially as we try to understand history in our time? Hardly. Then do these classic stories have no value? Is our faithing built on sand? Not at all! The stories have great value when one takes the time and makes the leap to understand them as poetry. Remember, something definable, maybe measurable, lies, lurks, beckons behind the poem. Some real people, just like you and me, only a long time ago, reaching out to the ends of their own being, recalled, sang, and/or wrote these stories.

Remember also, if I want to encounter the text, the text must also encounter me; I must find myself in the text. Anytime we face a scripture, we must be prepared to be faced. A dialectic conversation occurs if a word between God and me happens. So I start reading the creation stories in Genesis 1 and 2. Using the best linguistic tools I have and that I choose to use, I am persuaded I am reading neither science nor history. A few hundred years ago I perhaps could have read the narrative both as science and history, as fact. I cannot in honesty read Genesis 1 and 2 as science. Some people can; I cannot. The overwhelming weight of science persuades me that Genesis 1 and 2 fail the test of describing how creation came into being. I readily confess that science is still working on the how of that one, but the details in early Genesis do not get it.

Genesis also fails the history test by any modern-day measure of history. What's left? Much indeed. The overwhelming evidence of the human story as encountered in Genesis confirms a longer, more involved, infinitely more nuanced saga of how we humans got to where we are today.

A large body of linguistic and biblical studies over the past couple hundred years suggests the Genesis story of creation came from carefully nurtured and orally repeated folklore stories from the ancient Middle East. Exactly how the Genesis stories, especially the first eleven chapters in the Bible, came together embraces several theories, but the experts generally agree that ancient Jewish scholars used the hard times of the Babylonian exile of the Jews in the sixth century BCE to collect and refine much of what became the early narratives of the Old Testament from antiquity until the fall of Jerusalem in 622 BCE. The aim seems to be to offer the downcast exiles a national epic to assure them their Yahweh had not abandoned them. Do not despair, the sages implored, even though you have suffered devastating defeat and demoralization. Your life as a unique people of God is not over, despite the ravages of war that laid waste to Jerusalem, enslaved your leaders, and destroyed the temple traced to King Solomon. Imagine how we would feel if the terrorists of 9/11 had succeeded in leveling the White House or the U.S. Capitol, killed our leaders, or carried the leaders of the nation into Babylon (Iraq)?

For instance, behind the creation stories in Genesis, one finds some obvious facts. The sun, moon, rivers, oceans, animals, and humans do exist. Just look around. How did all this happen? A really good question of itself. Even though our ancient ancestors may not have yet known how to capture words in symbols they could write down, they were not dummies. They had curiosity. What about life, birth, death, food to eat? What about storms and good people and bad people? If it had not occurred to them to take a piece of charcoal and write their thoughts and questions on scraped and cleaned animal skin, they could sing, and they did. They could chant, and they did. They noticed that the craggy old woman of thirty-five summers had an uncanny way of recounting the tribe's lore in an absolutely enchanting, riveting way. So on nights when the weather was decent or on days that held special signifi-cance, the leader of the clan would invite her to tell again the story of how the moon came to hang in the night sky or why the rivers teemed with fish or how we humans got here in the first place. Believe me, those are basic questions we humans have pondered for eons—fundamental, existentialist inquiries. So even though the Genesis creation stories are neither science nor history, they address, if not answer, fundamental questions.

Our Hebrew ancestor/poets, exiled in Babylon, struggling for meaning, took the campfire stories to a new level, spinning them into soaring sagas of hope and triumph. Yahweh, they sang, their God, is the creator, the author of all that is. That reach became the quantum poetic, rhapsodic leap for our religious forebears. Did they take the stories literally? Literal was probably not a thought category for them. The truth they sought to convey transcended what we call history or science, categories they had not yet constructed. That pre-cellphone thought category is extremely difficult for us in the twenty-first century to grasp. We tend to be linear in our thinking. Our Hebrew ancestors wanted to assure the demoralized exiles that Yahweh had not been defeated by the unbelieving, marauding Babylonians. Not so fast, declared the teachers among the exiles to the exiles! Not only was Yahweh not defeated; he ruled the world as creator of the world and all in it. Do not "weep by the waters of Babylon." Yahweh yet rules and reigns supreme.

Within the other early Genesis narratives bits of history probably exist. Murders like that of Cain and Abel do happen. Great epic journeys like that of Abraham and Sarah occur. Why? Devastating floods occur. Are the gods angry? If their Yahweh created human beings, does Yahweh now have second thoughts? Offspring constantly go astray and disappoint, even anger, their parents. The campfire stories, the litanies recited at sacred moments framed their communal lives, bringing the people in closer proximity to the Holy, as the ancient Celts said, to "thin places" through which the seeker could enter and experience the transcendent in a new way. It is fruitless to search for the garden of Eden. It never existed as coordinates on a map. The garden of Eden flourishes any time, any place when people live in harmony with one another and with God. Humans foul the fullness of the garden then and now. Humans pay the price for their rebellion against the balance of the created order then and now.

Remember, "It may not have happened exactly like we have it here, but it's true anyway." Poetry!

CHAPTER EIGHT
Faithing and Imagination

Somewhere along the way I picked up the mantra that philosophy in its myriad iterations is the ongoing human attempt to understand life in general. Library shelves around the world groan under the weight of books of philosophy. From the time we began to walk around upright, we humans have puzzled over the meaning of life. The final, definitive issues of the meaning of life never stay settled. Invariably, when one wades through these tomes of human wisdom, the writer starts where some other sage has left off. Often, the given philosopher will go through the already published essay or book on his desk line by line. He will agree with portions of what she has written. He will disagree with parts of it. Then there is the inevitable "but." Philosophy is never finished because human life is never finished. About the time you think you have it figured out, some new wrinkle in the human experience pops up.

"What's the use?" you might be tempted to exclaim, throwing your hands up in the air. The "use" is that many of us are forever and anon curious about our own lives and the lives of others near and far, so we keep at it.

The same primordial pursuit applies to theology—that is, talk about God, gods, the Other, the Holy, Allah, etc. At the same time that we humans have tried to piece together a meaningful whole about life, we have likewise tried to have the same ongoing conversation about God or whatever or whomever we consider ultimate.

Further, it helps me realize that all philosophy and all theology are human constructs. At best, they are all approximations. As I have said previously, for these basic reasons it is the height of arrogance and folly to say, "*This* is it!" And it is likewise the height of hubris to insist that your way is the only way to anything, certainly the meaning of life and to the meaning of God.

For instance, Walter Isaacson in his excellent book *Innovators* describes the evolution of the digital age in which we now live and the electronic means by which I write these lines. The overriding point he makes for me comes as he describes how one person's breakthrough discoveries laid the foundation for the next layer of astounding discoveries and breakthroughs. Human history moves forward with never-ending "Yes, buts…" or "She got it right as far as she went. Now, I take it to a new level." This steadily spiraling upward (I think it's upward) persuades me that we humans are not done with anything. Uncle Sam, don't close the patent office just yet!

So I go for poetry and imagination. I talked about poetry in the last chapter. Close on the heels of poetry is imagination, maybe two sides of the same coin. With flights of imagination, we can posit the (make that *a*) meaning of life and God. For sure, as I engage in this journey of poetry and imagination, I want to make a concerted effort to underpin both my poetry and imagination with all the solid, dependable information I can collect. I want to try to inform poetry and imagination yet honestly to confess that all my best efforts are stabs, thrusts, approximations, metaphors. Hence, the turn to poetry and imagination.

Imagining God

As I move into the imagination phase of this conversation, I want to imagine God, more about the Bible, certainly Jesus. With poetic imagination I want to peer a bit into my future.

The best one can do is imagine God, while I readily confess I really cannot imagine God. Remember, language is all we possess to talk about and think about God. We use human words shaped by eons of human experience. As words are mundane expressions of our humanness, so will be our conversation about God. Mundane, definable, measurable, yet in the same breath agree that all our God-talk is approximation, metaphor, culturally cast, limited. As marvelous as is the gift of language, recall always the limitations of language. So our castings around for and about God are essentially limited. This means to me to put aside hubris and parochialism in our pontifications about the Other, the Holy. Certainly, claim your own relationship with your God; just leave me existential room for my relationship with her/them. I am emphatically a God person. At the same time I bow before the wondrous, compelling, evocative mystery of such an affirmation.

In 2015 the U.S. Supreme Court agreed to marriage equality nationwide. While I applauded the decision, minions of my fellow religionists came unglued at the ruling. Politicians pronounced the end of American civilization.

Preachers promised to bar their church doors against any of "them" who dared come for a ceremony. And, by the way, some bakeries do not want to make a wedding cake for a same-sex couple, a situation the Supreme Court has agreed to consider (I cannot imagine a gay couple wanting to engage such a minister or his domain or a baker for their big moment of union). This same-sex marriage thing was simply not God's plan for us humans, they dogmatized! I could go with them if they said something like, "I don't think same-sex marriage is a good idea. I don't think God thinks this is the best way." However, most of these folks were sure what God liked, approved of, inscribed in the human DNA code. Their theological hubris and naïveté choke me. A few days ago, a noted preacher of a huge Texas church declared that God had given the president "authority" to vanquish North Korea's dictator. Talk about over the top; that's it! Remember, they made the same sweeping pronouncements on the ownership of slaves or on the physics of the solar system.

When I think and talk about God, I offer a synthesis from several writers, especially from Marcus Borg, that works for me. Borg says in a variety of ways in several of his books, especially in *Meeting Jesus Again for the First Time*. "The word *God* refers to the sacred at the center of existence, the holy mystery that is all around us and within us. God is the non-material ground and source and presence in which, as Paul says, 'we live and move and have our being.'" He says, "One does not so much believe in God as to experience this sacred, this experiential reality at the heart of existence."

I say again, God is as air to humans. God is as water to fish. God is as gravity to the universe. God is primal energy. Dr. Borg and other scholars of his stripe use a word I like to employ as I talk about God—panentheism. That means to me everything is in God but God is not in everything. Pantheism, a classic notion, suggests that God and the material universe are one and the same. By saying everything is in God, panentheism, I can get nearer to that enormous notion of God. But I do not go for the pedestrian notion that God and the beautiful, fragrant lilacs on my bushes in the spring are one and the same. The lilacs are expressions of the stupendous created order. The lilacs are not God.

If this rather rarefied and even fuzzy notion of God does not work for you, so be it. You let me have my imaginings about God, and I will surely let you have yours. Don't insist that I sign on to yours, and I will not badger you to sign on to mine.

I will emphatically insist that our collective gods, to have any integrity, must promote, encourage, honor, and represent the basic human values of love, freedom, and justice. At this writing the world is attempting to deal with a growing host of blood-thirsty killers in the name of Islam. And they must be dealt with. Responsible Muslims worldwide repudiate the radicals, the thoroughly bad apples, within their religious fold. In the days after the terrible shooting in Chattanooga in 2015 by a boy from a Muslim-American family, Franklin Graham, the fire-breathing son of Billy, ranted that the United States should henceforth bar all Muslims. Talk about cruel rhetoric! Many of us ached as Donald Trump said we should ban all Muslims from coming into our country.

Take a deep breath now. Before we get too high and mighty about evil Islam, let's remember our own bloody history as Christians. Stories in the earlier portions of Hebrew Scripture, our Old Testament, paint a rampaging, bloody Yahweh. Portions of the New Testament and strains of Christian theology seem to say that God wanted Jesus to die the inscrutably painful death on the cross as some sort of payback for human sin. Bands of Christian crusaders (c. 1095–1291) sanctioned by various popes marched and thrived on human blood. Wars of religion ravaged Europe for centuries. Women and men in the Golden Age of Elizabethan England were martyred in cauldrons of boiling oil for not agreeing to this or that nuance about Holy Communion. We Americans hung witches on Boston Common. Ku Klux Klan klaverns with a burning cross as backdrop ravaged and lynched southern blacks in the not-too-distant past. White supremacists and neo-Nazis also know what the inside of Christian churches look like. Unfortunately, the tragic saga goes on and on.

So let's try to agree on the basics of the Holy we imagine: deities that generate the primal energies of love, freedom, and justice. I do not have space in my psyche for lesser gods. The gods of the Klan, of Westboro Church, of Isis are anathema to me! If we think the God of love, justice, and freedom is a Wussy, try consistently to become a person of love or justice or freedom and find out what a tough assignment you have chosen.

Christian Wiman has powerful lines about God that get at the poetry and imagination I am suggesting. He says many of us experience "the burn of being that drives us out of ourselves [to] the persistent gravity of the ghost called God."[12] Stupendous! I wish I could have thought up that poetic, imaginative way to think about God.

Imagining the Bible

Now that we have "settled" the God thing, let's move on to talk imaginatively about the Bible. Recall, the Bible is a human book. Say what you will about divine inspiration, people wrote what we have in the Bible—for that matter all the books we humans write, including those we call "Holy Writ." In my imagination, for instance, the Bible has come to include mental pictures, say, of an Isaiah in the sixth century BCE struggling with the hopes and pains of his scrappy Hebrew family, friends, and neighbors. He tries to push through misplaced conceptions of Yahweh that falsely persuade the people Yahweh would not let harm come to them no matter the ferocity of barbarians at their gates. Generations of earthy, painfully honest poets like Isaiah, Jeremiah, the psalmists, and Ezekiel rhapsodized and complained bitterly about the totally unpredictable ways of their Holy One. In one line of the psalms, the Almighty is steadfast love. In the next line the poet, nearly driven to distraction, demands to know why the Lord has abandoned his faithful servant to the ravages of a godless enemy. Remember that often the enemy was simply a nearby "kinglet" upset because the "people of Yahweh" had decided to go on their annual spring rampage, destroying crops, stealing livestock, and ravaging women in the next "county."

Thus, the Bible is a magisterial, honest book by and about a small collection of human beings in a tiny backwater land trying to figure out who God is and what they have to do to get along with God and one another. For me, as my years have fled toward eighty, the Bible has become a grand collection of altogether human words about God. Rather than the word from God to us mortals, the Bible is our existential human word to and about God. My imaginative encounter with the Bible persuades me some of the writers put words in God's mouth. Sometimes the words put in God's mouth were harsh, such as when God told Joshua to wipe out the village of Ai (Josh 8). At other times, poets put words in God's mouth that sang and soared: "Let justice roll on like a mighty river; righteousness like a never-failing stream" (Amos 5:24).

In an ongoing effort to keep our imaginings about the Bible in focus, recall that what we describe as the Old Testament came into being over a long period of time, at least a thousand years. Also remember that for thirty-nine "books" in the canon, hundreds of writings, poems, sagas that people read and revered in their time did not make the final cut. For a variety of good and capricious reasons, they were left out of the canon.

The Christian part of the Bible, what we call the New Testament, came into its present form over a shorter period of time, maybe a hundred years from Paul's letters, as early as the 40s CE, to the book of Revelation into the 100s CE. A bevy of New Testament scholars now want to extend parts of the New Testament well into the second Christian century. It was into the fourth Christian century before the bishops finally agreed more or less on what we have. Then Martin Luther in the sixteenth century did not want the Old Testament book of Esther or the New Testament book of James in the canon. For me, then, it is a fundamental mistake of Christian faith and theology to insist on a literal reading of the Bible, especially in every instance. The Bible is magnificent poetry generated by imagination flung inward, outward, and upward toward the Holy, the Other, the Beyondness, the wondrous "burn" of our human effort to relate, to grasp the "gravity of the ghost we call God."

Imagining Jesus.

Jesus is central to my faithing as eighty bears down on me. In other parts of this memoir, I have talked about and around Jesus. It's time now to focus. In discussing the narratives of the Old Testament, I focused on them as poetry. I have pointed to theology as poetry. Here, as I pick up my idea of imagination, I will focus on Jesus. I confess an inability to talk about God only in the most esoteric, poetic way. I can approach Jesus with more historical confidence.

Recall that I grew up in the American South, thinking (without really thinking) that Christ was Jesus' last name, like Maddox for me. I was well into my time as a pastor, with years of biblical and theological studies behind me, before it actually, viscerally dawned on me that Christ was a title of honor given to Jesus by his post-Easter followers. *Christ* is a Greek translation of a Hebrew word for *messiah*. A few Old Testament characters were awarded the title "messiah," or "special leader," making it plain that the early post-Easter Jesus people did not invent the title; they appropriated it, baptized it, and decorated Jesus with the honored title, now, their faith persuaded them, raised by God.

These days when I hear people today talk about the life of Christ, the death of Christ, or the advent of Christ, I wince. What they are really talking about is the life of Jesus, the death of Jesus, or the ministry of Jesus. Christ had no human life! Christ did not die. In fact, Jesus as Christ only started living (and that in the faith-inspired imagination of his followers) after he died on the cross. Our ancestors who walked in the ways of Jesus after he was off the scene had pivotal yet inaccessible experiences they identified with Jesus beyond his death. The empty tomb sagas evidently emerged from these moments our ancestors had with the crucified-but-now-with-God Jesus. Remember, other notable figures such as kings and emperors had a way of coming back after they died. Why not Jesus, this grand, godly, gifted, unselfish, wise, caring man from Galilee? As previously noted, years later, the so-called Gospel of Peter (150–200 CE) only reinforced the developing Easter empty tomb story.

I have said in other places that I was never comfortable preaching about Christ. I did not understand the reason for my discomfort until much later into my ministry. I realize now that for years and years I had been looking for Jesus. It was not until I had that Damascus road experience in 1992 when I first read Marcus Borg's *Meeting Jesus Again for the First Time* that new light began to illuminate murky places in my mind. With Borg as guide, I went through my own "thin place" into a relationship, an experiential reality, with a historical figure with whom I existentially continue to interact at eighty.

My brief snatches in the 1970s with the demythologizing writings of Rudolf Bultmann whetted my Jesus appetite, but I did not take the time to pursue further that line of thought. From my earliest years I regarded myself as an existentialist when it came to faith; that is, I wanted to encounter faith in a serious, personal way that reached way inside. Thanks to that grand course in graduate school when the professor urged the new hermeneutic on us, I began to put together the second part of the equation: to encounter and to be encountered. I was onto something important in my own journey, but life moved on too fast for me to pay much fresh attention to the rest of me.

Soon after I finished my doctoral degree at Candler School of Emory University in 1975, I got swept up into the dizzy world of the Jimmy Carter campaign and then White House and, from there, for eight years, onto another aspect of the national stage as executive director of Americans United for the Separation of Church and State. Not until 1992, when I became pastor of the Briggs Memorial Baptist Church in Bethesda, Maryland, did I find the space to pay fresh attention to more of my own personal story. Frankly, I did not give Jesus much of my time and thought from the late 1970s until 1992. As I left Americans United for Briggs, I said I wanted time to write and reflect. Little did I know what I would write and about what I would reflect. The writing and reflecting found me, I am happy to say.

I have to go back to some earlier parts of this personal story at this point before I can pick up my flights of imagination related to Jesus. As a younger minister reared almost entirely in the Southern Baptist culture, for my part, as I have previously noted, I lacked the academic and emotional tools to deal with my own Jesus ambiguities. As I previously noted, the powerful Baptist Christian Life Seminars produced by the late Dr. Foy Valentine were seminal for me. These annual events focused on critical issues of race, politics, social justice, changing sexual attitudes, family, and much more. They provided me substantive intellectual and spiritual sustenance in and through graduate school in those days from the middle 1960s until the late 1970s. Dr. Valentine's seminars offered a safe place to push myself.

By the early 1980s I did know the Baptist ground where I had stood for most of my young years had experienced seismic shifts. The larger Southern Baptist Convention had always been theologically conservative. Until the 1980s the Southern Baptist tent was big enough to make room for a wide range of social and theological mindsets. I have stated about how basically unexciting the seminary was for me. Still, I felt at home. With the emergence of the ultra-conservative climate in the country that brought Ronald Reagan to the White House, the Southern Baptist tent began to shrink decidedly. By the close of the 1980s, no room remained for the likes of me. Reflective of the theological sea change, the Southern Baptist Convention began to splinter, with small groups pulling away to form more moderate, progressive, less restrictive frameworks.

In Southern Baptist life the national organization, headquartered in Nashville, Tennessee, owned the six seminaries located in key cities across the country. State Baptist organizations, conventions, primarily in the South and West, owned the denominational colleges and universities. In the course of these upheavals in Southern Baptist life, two major changes occurred in higher education. The larger state, Baptist-owned colleges and universities exercised clauses in their charters to break official ties with the state Baptist organizations lest the new conservatism insinuate itself into local conventions and choke off curiosity and any measure of academic freedom from the schools. Many now-independent Baptist colleges recognized the profound change in theological education and set about to create divinity schools directly related to the universities. Though generally theologically conservative, these new schools offered much more freedom and diversity, including a place for women to become ordained pastors of churches. Progress, yes. Still, for my part very few of these new seminaries have caught up with the times, but they will especially, in agreeing to welcome clergy who are openly gay. At any rate, the times they were a-changing. I attended my last annual meeting of the Southern Baptist Convention in about 1988 and decided I would waste no more time and money that way. I was disappointed, frustrated, pained to see what had happened to the national institution, with all its human warts, that had nurtured so many of us. But the die was cast.

Fortunately, Briggs Memorial Baptist Church had never been pulled into the restrictive attitudes of the Southern Baptist Convention. With no fanfare the church had ordained a woman to ministry when such a move was practically unheard of. The church had also ordained women to serve as deacons, in Baptist life an office of high responsibility. To this day, the typical Southern Baptist church will not ordain women as clergy or deacons. Southern Baptist churches that have followed their conscience and put women in places of ministerial responsibility have been "disfellowshipped," booted out of many local, state, and national bodies. These days, in addition to the role of women in the church, the involvement of gays and lesbians in the church has become another ugly litmus test. Recently, a California Southern Baptist church tried to thread the homosexual needle, saying they had found no definitive biblical proscription to that lifestyle; further, they simply wanted to study the issue in a less charged atmosphere. The Southern Baptist Convention of California would not tolerate a "third way." The larger body broke ties with the local Baptist church that simply wanted to embrace the time-honored principle for Baptist churches to exercise local autonomy. Fortunately, the Briggs Church, while having ties to both Southern Baptists and American Baptists, connected most closely with the local District of Columbia Baptist Convention, which had refused to violate local church autonomy, thus avoiding the divisive culture wars. Eventually, sad to say, the Southern Baptist Convention caught on to this intolerable measure of freedom, shook its collective finger at the liberty-loving psyche of the local convention, and cut off funds essential to an effective Baptist ministry in Washington, DC.

As I went to Briggs Church in 1992, I sensed the independence, freedom, and farsightedness of the congregation. Though small in numbers when I became pastor, due to years of attrition and shifting demographics, the church had strength of spirit and the financial resources to conduct a vigorous ministry. I likewise sensed among them a willingness to give me room to take another step in my own faithing journey, though I had no notion of the next iteration of the trip.

Another most important aspect of ministry occurred as Linda and I took leadership in the Briggs Church. Washington, DC, at that particular moment embraced a host of young people working on Capitol Hill, many of whom had Baylor University connections. Thanks to the drawing power of some of the more charismatic among those Baylor people, our church became a mecca for about thirty of these super-bright, energetic, open-minded people who were ready and willing for a new church experience.

Tim Tutt was among them. He had graduated from Baylor in 1991 and gone to work on Capitol Hill for a Texas congressman. Within a few weeks of attending Briggs, he became our unofficial lay worship leader. It helped that Amy Prichard, also of Baylor, had already volunteered to help as outreach leader for the church. Tim, I surmise, had long had his eye on Amy, and their time at Briggs solidified the relationship, resulting in their marriage in 1994. After about a year of involvement in the church, Tim came to a long-delayed decision to pursue ministry as a calling. The congressman agreed for Tim to continue working and also to attend part time a new progressive Baptist seminary in Richmond, Virginia, in a four-year rather than the traditional three-year regimen.

Within a short time the church asked Tim to become an official part of the staff on a part-time basis. Tim's own studies brought a freshness to me that meshed completely with my own reinvention as a Jesus person. By the grace of God, an enduring friendship was forged to the point that after eleven years in a United Church of Christ congregation in Austin, Texas, Tim and Amy moved back to Bethesda in 2012 where he is now pastor of our Westmoreland Congregational United Church of Christ. Who could ask for more?

Now, with this bit of refresher history as context, I will gather up my previous conversations about Jesus and me and that host of courageous scholars who had set out to reintroduce Jesus of Nazareth to the Christian world. By now you realize Marcus Borg lit the fire at my own burning bush experience with Jesus. Dr. Borg, who taught religion in a state university, had grown up in a traditional midwestern Lutheran church. Along the way his theological work prompted him to take seriously the life and ministry of Jesus of Nazareth, the Jesus of history. Borg became part of a rapidly expanding cadre of scholars teaching primarily in safe departments of religion in state or private universities, shielded from the vagaries of denominational theological witch hunts. These religiously oriented academics decided to learn all they could about the living, breathing man, Jesus of Nazareth.

In the late eighteenth and unfolding nineteenth centuries, some New Testament scholars, many from Germany, began to put their minds together to find out what they could of this person Jesus who had so shaped world history. Not a few of these brave souls suffered the slings and arrows of incensed prelates and an irate lay and clerical constituency, stifling but not stopping their pursuits. The Jesus of Nazareth genie was out of the bottle, meaning these studies moved inexorably ahead, if in fits and starts. The Jesus of history studies came crashing down in 1906. The theological giant Albert Schweitzer determined that nothing of substance could be known of the historical Jesus. We could know the Christ of faith he inveighed, but we could not know the Jesus of history. Rudolf Bultmann, in the first half of the twentieth century, basically agreed with Schweitzer. But moving at his own pace, Bultmann developed the ground-shaking existential approach to the Christ of faith. Building on much that had gone before, by the middle of the twentieth century, scholars employed new tools for studying the archeology, sociology, and anthropology of such history-shrouded figures. The Jesus of history gradually came into focus.

Marcus Borg, John Dominic Crossan, John Shelby Spong, Elaine Pagels, and many more scholars began to dig deeper and deeper into the social and cultural milieu that could have produced a figure like Jesus. In the midst of this ferment, Dr. Robert Funk of the California Westar Institute led in the creation of the Jesus Seminar, whose goal it was to take Jesus of history studies to a new academic level. As one would expect, Dr. Borg and his colleagues met stiff resistance as they began to put a human face on Jesus. For my part I will forever be indebted to them for their courageous, groundbreaking work. Drawing from their labors as historians—adding in the seminal work of the likes of Carl Jung, the existentialism of Bultmann, the boundarylessness of Eagleman, and the cumulative tradition paradigm of Cantwell Smith—I found the Jesus for whom I had searched since my college days.

Now I need to invite you to join me in furthering my imaginative, existential connection with Jesus of Nazareth. I want to introduce two classically dependable but different-sounding rubrics about Jesus: the pre-Easter Jesus and the post-Easter Jesus.

The pre-Easter Jesus is the Jewish man from Nazareth living under the double tyranny of a politico/conservative Jewish religious system that had managed to lose much of its vibrancy. The other tyranny was the chokehold of occupation by imperial Rome. These two facts of history form the larger anthropological and historical context for the pre-Easter Jesus.

The canonical Easter narratives tell the story of the resurrection of Jesus from the tomb after his crucifixion, the post-Easter Jesus. With the work and writings of Paul, these narratives, told in variations only in the four Gospels, stand out as the watershed events in the formation of the Jesus movement that became the Christian church. The canonical Easter empty tomb story, told first in the Gospel of Mark (about 70 CE), opens the New Testament narrative curtain on the post-Easter Jesus. The Gospels of Matthew, Luke (sometime after 80 CE), and John (about 90–120 CE) give the empty tomb stories. Remember, Paul, writing from about 40 to 60 CE, sings of the risen Christ but says nothing about the empty tomb. The pre-Easter Jesus has a mundane, if often overlooked history. The post-Easter Jesus is beyond history, a faith saga perpetuated through religious devotion and the unfolding, ever-developing cumulative Christian tradition.

Pre-Easter Jesus

I cannot begin to footnote what I want to lay out here. Numerous contemporary scholars, particularly Marcus Borg and John Dominic Crossan, have gifted me with much of what I want to put before you in the next few pages.

I am deeply indebted particularly to Marcus Borg who enabled me to meet Jesus again for the first time. Domnic Crossan provided invaluable insights especially in his book: *The Birth of Christianity*. Beyond these two a host of some of the brightest, most earnest and spiritually driven scholars have also enriched this effort. The past years have afforded me the opportunity to spend time with several of these noted scholars, convincing me even more of their genuine desire to make Jesus real in our time.

The pre-Easter Jesus points us to the living, walking, talking, laughing, crying, hurting, compelling, driven, public, yet reclusive man. This gifted man in all likelihood was born and grew up in the tiny northern village of Nazareth in the Galilee region of the Roman-occupied province of Judea, a few miles from the large Roman/Greek/Jewish city of Sepphoris.[13]

Substantially, what we know about the man Jesus comes from the four New Testament Gospels. These short "books" are not biographies of Jesus. My persuasion is that they are stitched-together memories of friends and initial followers of Jesus. If Jesus died in about 30 CE, Mark, the earliest of the Gospels to have survived the ravages of time, seems to have come into existence some forty years after Jesus' time. None of the four Gospel writers was an eyewitness to anything he wrote about. Nothing is really known of the authors of the books. The titles are emerged legend certainly not from any attribution by the actual authors.

Where did the Gospel writers get their information? Theories abound. Was "Mark" a protégé of Peter? Did he write from Rome? Did he ever visit Judea? Was Luke, apparently the only non-Jewish Gospel author, a traveling companion with Paul? Legend says Matthew is the tax collector/disciple Jesus enlisted. Was John one of the original disciples? Is he the same John credited with writing the soaring, poetic book of Revelation? Engaging, ancient anonymity shrouds all four Gospel writers. How historically accurate are they? No one knows. Similar themes about Jesus run through Mark, Matthew, and Luke, suggesting the writers had some access to one another's materials but probably not to each other personally. In recent decades New Testament scholars have posited a prior document from which the Synoptic Gospels might have drawn information about Jesus. John was written some years later, maybe even into the second Christian century, when the Jesus movement had become more fully entrenched in pockets of the vast Roman Empire. His book has a distinctly different take on Jesus: no parables, long speeches purportedly from Jesus, a different chronology at some key points. Frankly, we could spend a vast amount of time exploring the differences and similarities of the four Gospels. I hope what I am saying whets your own appetite for much further study.

Win, lose, or draw, the canonical Gospels are the best we have on the living, walking, talking Jesus of Nazareth. So far, no original manuscripts of any of the New Testament documents have surfaced. Some very ancient manuscripts, copies of copies, do exist, but they date from well into the subsequent centuries. I hasten to say many more so-called Gospels existed, parts of which continue to surface and are available for study. They are known from second- and thirdhand references to them in other later writings. Off and on through the centuries, valuable early documents about Jesus do surface that offer both similar and different takes on Jesus and the movement that developed around and after his time in Judea.

Remember always, Paul's letters, written some years before the four Gospels, give practically no biographical information about Jesus. Pauline faith statements abound but no history. Where did Paul get his information? Where does his elevated Christology find its genesis? Ongoing questions. Avoid dogmatic assertions about any aspects of this grand but foggy history. One can make exciting guesses but very few incontrovertible declarations. With considerable certainty it can be insisted that the Gospels, as well as Paul's letters, are aimed primarily at the non-Jewish population of the Near Eastern (Asia Minor) portion of the Roman Empire under the Caesars toward the end of what we call the first Christian century and into the second.

The pervasive thread that runs through all four Gospels, Acts, and Paul's letters is that Jesus lived for a while in Roman-occupied Galilee and died on a Roman cross, probably in Jerusalem. No serious historian doubts the historical existence of Jesus, and they are nearly unanimous in his death by crucifixion.

So here's where imagination comes into play. Let me be clear, not silly, willy-nilly imagination. I engage imagination that comes from serious, ongoing scholarly study that provides promising clues to the multiple blanks in the historical life of Jesus of Nazareth. I go to my hall-of-fame scholars who have devoted now decades to the reverent, careful, if often unsettling investigation into Jesus of Nazareth. For me they have offered exciting possibilities to better experience Jesus of Nazareth as a living human being. Hence, I find myself in good company with them. (See the bibliography of the women and men who have offered much richness to me.)

A thematic, imaginative, and informed framework proposed by Marcus Borg gets to the essence of the Jesus of history, the pre-Easter Jesus, for me. Remember, the broad outline of the life of the pre-Easter Jesus is what can be gathered, collected, surmised, carefully imagined about the Jesus of datable, mundane history who lived in Roman-occupied Galilee from approximately 4 BCE to about 30 CE. Recent scholarship pointing toward an analysis of cross-cultural anthropology provides many helpful clues in creating a gestalt of Jesus of Nazareth. Approximations. Carefully wrought educated guesses. Sure.

Here, I offer Marcus Borg's sketch of the pre-Easter Jesus that captured my imagination then and holds it for me still:

- Jesus was thoroughly Jewish; he was born, lived, and died as a Jew of the Roman/Herodian era. He sought to revitalize the Jewish traditions of his own time.
- By any measure he was an extraordinary man. He inspired deep devotion among those who knew him best and walked most closely with him. He fired their hopes, energies, courage, and imagination.
- Jesus was a Spirit person. He was full of God. He mediated the sacred. He walked with and lived in God. He went through "thin places" in his relationship with God.
- Jesus was a teacher of wisdom—a wisdom that was often subversive to the accepted social order. He was a master of the parable and aphorism. Many contemporary scholars say the parables come nearest to the authentic voice of the historic Jesus.
- Jesus was a social prophet. In the mode of the Hebrew prophets, he challenged the social order. He taught and served in constant conflict with political and religious authorities. He challenged the elitism of his time.
- Jesus was a movement founder. The movement he fostered sought to revitalize the Jewishness of his time. He challenged the status quo. The movement eventually became the Christian church.
- Jesus of Nazareth did not make messianic claims for himself; he always pointed everyone to God. These messianic claims from the Gospels, especially from the Gospel of John, came from his followers after the

crucifixion out of admiration and love for Jesus. As the decades rolled by—with the locus of the movement shifting from Judea to the larger Roman world—the Jesus movement, now largely Gentile/non-Jewish, increasingly draped divinity around him to position Jesus favorably in the imagination of the Roman world in which they all lived.[14]

I am aware that this sketch of Jesus challenges what many of us have heard and believed about him for a long time. You may well choose to ignore all that I am experiencing about Jesus. I hasten to say that many scholars of reputation question the Jesus of history approach. Conversely, many Western Christians have, in a variety of ways, embraced this understanding of Jesus and find, with me, that it makes sense in the light of what we are discovering about first-century life.

Post-Easter Jesus

The post-Easter Jesus became an experiential reality to a growing body of followers of Jesus after his death. Like Paul on the Damascus road, countless Jesus people across the ages have had their own moments with what they understood to be the risen Jesus. These moments could not be captured on film, but no one should deny the importance of these experiences to the individual. Who am I to say it never happened to you? I go back to Eagleman's idea that with the power of the human brain, anything is possible. We must always test the moment against the Jesus who loved, served, and gave himself for his friends. For twenty-first-century followers of Jesus, myself included, Jesus remains an experiential reality. At the same time, I can identify much more fully with the living, breathing Jesus of Nazareth. My understanding of this Jesus of history becomes the filter for my personal experiential encounters with the living Jesus. For me this elision between the Jesus of history and the Christ of faith puts in manageable perspective numerous bothersome debates: birth stories, miracles, and healings ascribed to Jesus; unanswerable questions about the resurrection and the human and divine natures of Jesus, all of which have vexed theologians for centuries.

The immediate followers of Jesus lived in and out of two powerful experiences with Jesus. They experienced him as the man from Galilee, the pre-Easter Jesus. After his death, they experienced him, they proclaimed, as raised by the power of God, hence the post-Easter Jesus. The post-Easter Jesus lived beyond the crucifixion in the experiences of a growing number of people who chose to open themselves to the experiential reality of the risen Jesus. The traditional view of Easter includes an empty tomb at the dawning of a Sunday morning on the outskirts of Jerusalem. For me the tomb is most likely not empty; still, Jesus lives on.

In no way does my experience with Jesus that deeply embraces Jesus of Nazareth stop with an encounter with Jesus the man from Galilee. I have come to embrace the post-Easter Jesus in ways, perhaps (I say *perhaps* comparable to what those friends and followers who did know him face to face experienced in the years after the crucifixion). In their inner beings, in the depths of their existence, these Jesus people in the 60s and 70s CE and into the second and third centuries experienced Jesus living on. Were they fooling themselves? Were they choosing to have a relationship with this risen Jesus? Maybe yes, on both counts. But the experiences, whatever they were, motivated them to build a powerful, generous, compassionate movement that has blessed humankind for 2,000 years.

Herein, I return to my own cluster of metaphors that help me internalize my feeling and experiences with Jesus. Increasingly, I open myself to Carl Jung's powerful concept of collective unconsciousness, his concept of archetype. My brain (my psyche) is connected to Jesus just as it is connected to a vast amount of the totality of human experience before me.

Then comes Cantwell Smith's cumulative tradition. For 2,000 years now my ancestors who likewise chose to connect with Jesus in infinite ways, built steadily, inexorably, a Christian tradition they have passed on to me and that I, in turn, continue to build and will pass on to my own spiritual heirs. And then comes David Eagleman's seminal fresh discoveries of the powers of the human brain, which points out that anything is possible, if not in the past, if not now, certainly into the future.

Can I prove what I am saying? No, but I do not need to. I have invested decades of beckoning study, examined many crosscurrents, considered, accepted, and laid aside many ideas to get me where I am. In short, for my part I did not come here by the seat of my pants. At some important junctures in this process, I made my own existential leaps. I came to some important "Yes" moments for myself.

Wait just a minute, you might be sputtering! What about the miracles; the great "I am" statements Jesus made; healing, walking on water, feeding thousands with a boy's lunch?

Jesus was a healer. Did he simply wave his hand over sick people and make them well, restore sight to blind eyes, cure a paralytic? Probably not. Some New Testament scholarship has suggested Jesus may have accumulated some medical training within the context of medicine in his day. Interesting possibility to me. Studies of the times in which Jesus lived have references to other healers.

Walking on water, feeding thousands, stilling a storm, telling his friends how to fill their empty fishnets? I have no trouble ascribing these stories to loving embellishments from devoted followers amazed at his insights into the needs and hurts of his friends. Try to get inside the stories of the so-called miracles. What do those flights of faith-filled imagination say about Jesus?

For instance, for the "I am" statements, especially in the Gospel of John, I offer the following imaginings. In regard to "believe in Jesus and find eternal life" statements in the Gospel of John (John 3:16; 14), let me give some ideas based on careful study of the book of John itself. Jesus probably did not say what John says he said. John wrote decades after Jesus was off the scene physically. He wrote into and out of his part of the developing tradition that could assert this exclusive assertion of Jesus as the only way to God. But there's more for me. I affirm that following in the way of the most compassionate dimensions of the Jesus tradition does lead to a quality of life that blesses and enriches—that "saves" us, if you will, from a life of emptiness, anger, and condemnation to a life of hope and promise. As we become people of Spirit, go about healing the wounds of humanity, live as compassionate human beings, go up against entrenched power, we find a quality of human life that's worth all the effort we invest in the living of the Jesus way.

We also need to pay attention to what Jesus did say about the kingdom of God. I doubt if Jesus puzzled long over the existence of God. For Jesus, God was present, real in his understanding of real. Jesus emphasized the idea of kingdom. For Jesus the kingdom of God was a present reality. It was not something *yet* to come; it had come *already*. The kingdom of God for Jesus was not our mythologized idea of heaven, the golden city in the sky beyond this life. So it is easier for a camel to go through the eye of a needle than for a rich man to enter into the kingdom of God when we understand the kingdom as a way to live one's life, God's way, on a day-by-day basis. I want to understand, grasp, live in terms of the kingdom as now, God among us, as a way of compassion, healing, caring, tending to the earth, mediating distributive justice, and more. Sure it's hard for the rich man and any of us to go through that needle's eye if we live only for ourselves with little or no regard for those attitudes that Jesus exemplified. Women and men up and down the economic ladder can ignore the values that Jesus promoted as central to living in terms of the kingdom of God in any era and miss the exuberance of living as kingdom people.

What does this existential approach do for me? It fits with my twenty-first-century worldview of humanity, the best of what we humans can become. It fits with a huge body of scholarship about the development of the New Testament, the development of the movement that became the church that became Christianity. I do not have to squeeze the Gospels and what we think we can know about the life of Jesus into a rigid mold that refuses to take seriously any of those studies.

This view of Jesus and Christianity fits my imagining of the way religions develop and unfold. It frees me from insisting that Christianity alone is the way to God. If God is the heart and soul of the universe and all existence, it beggars the imagination that only the hyper-exclusive way of evangelical and Roman Catholic Christianity is the sole way for billions and billions of people on the earth to relate to the heart and soul of the universe. It also fits what we conclude that Jesus said and understood about himself—a man eager to relate fully to the Holy and serve people with all his being. Jesus as unique Son of God would come later in the imagination and adoration of a growing host of Jesus people living their version of Easter faith.

Did you follow much of Pope Francis's visit to the United States in the fall of 2015? Recovering from a bout of surgery, I piled down in my favorite chair in the den and followed closely his journey to America. He pushed his own church and the rest of us toward a larger, much more generous approach to religious inclusiveness. Without giving up his own tradition, he constant-ly embraced religious leaders from many perspectives. I hope Pope Francis survives the bashing from his more conservative colleagues. What he says and does will have a long and lasting shelf-life.

It took me a while to get to this liberated, no-boundaries point in life. Even after I "met Jesus again for the first time," I had much to puzzle through. At a Marcus Borg lecture at Washington's National Cathedral, I asked Dr. Borg, "What is different, say, between George Washington and Jesus? Washington, by any measure, was an outstanding human being. Why can't I believe in him in the same way I want to believe in Jesus?"

Dr. Borg did not give me an answer. Later, when I had two days with him when he went with Jim Wallis of Sojourners and me to meet in Plains with President Carter, I had a chance to go further into that question. I am not sure what Borg finally said, but I came out saying that at one level, there is no difference between putting one's faith in Washington and in Jesus. Quantitatively and qualitatively, Jesus is far more important to world history than Washington, though I have great respect and admiration for Washington. Along the way as I dug into Carl Jung's idea of collective unconscious and archetype, as I embraced Smith's cumulative tradition and Eagleman's possibilitarianism, I began to say that Jesus is part of me, but so is George Washington. As an American I am a Washington person. As a human being I am a Jesus person. I can learn from and appreciate Washington. My existential connection with Jesus fundamentally shapes my life.

It's clear the second most important figure in the development of the Jesus movement is Paul of Tarsus. Though he says he got his revelation about Jesus directly, at other points he refers to meetings with James, the brother of Jesus, and Peter. Something triggered Paul's initial fury at the developing Jesus movement. The fury turned to devotion after his encounter with what he imagined was the risen Jesus on the road to Damascus. From what he knew second hand of Jesus and his thorough knowledge of the Hebrew scriptures and the history of the Jewish people, Paul must have extrapolated, imagined, his developing theology, his Christology. As I have said previously, his was a work in progress. He certainly wanted Jews living outside the homeland and the non-Jews he met to come to faith in Jesus as the risen Christ of God, in some way the savior of the world. He seamlessly makes beautiful use of poetry and imagination to convey his assertion that the message he conveys trumpets none other than Jesus the Christ, the savior.

Who would have thought a courageous young Galilean preacher imagined a community in an unbrokered relationship with God? A brilliant, inordinately difficult scholar got knocked to his knees in a vision he imagined to be that Galilean preacher, grandly, in a flight of cosmic poetry (Philippians 2: 5-11, Roman 8:31-39), elevated by God to become the savior of the world. People caught in the maw of Roman imperialism imagined they could find freedom in life and hope for heaven in the embrace of this Galilean preacher as declared by a growing host of theological poets with Holy Spirit-charged imaginations.

Poetry and Imagination in Real Time

Moving ahead to our own time, what have poetry and imagination come to mean in my life, in the lives Linda and I have experienced together? As I said earlier, I am pushed back to days of yore, times when poetry and imagination, as such, were not on my personal radar. Well, not entirely. Miss Faith Porch, my English teacher that high school junior year I spent at Gordon Military College, required us to study and memorize some stanzas of American poetry. We memorized the closing lines of "Thanatopsis." I could recite "The Midnight Ride of Paul Revere," lines from "The Marshes of Glynn," all of "Annabel Lee," and more. I reveled in the poems and got a kick out of memorizing the lines and then reciting them in class. But poetry as a window into life, particularly theology, not yet. At this point, however, trying to put more pieces of my existential faithing in place, poetry and imagination have begun to come into delightfully fresh focus.

Imagination. Those YFC rallies I found so daunting did serve to nudge my untutored imagination to decide there had to be a better way to relate to God. I came to no lightning-flash discoveries, but the nudge to find my way became more pronounced. As is often the case, through nagging persistence the positive can emerge from the negative. The positive began to become clearer during those student years at Baylor University.

Dick Baker's song "His Way Mine." The Texas Baptist world I entered in 1955 was on the tapering end of the South-wide youth revival movement that had energized young preachers and musicians in the religious awakening after World War II. Billy Graham had burst on the national stage. The Baylor University rendering of this surge brought a host of bright young preachers and singers to the campus. Running through much of their singing and preaching was a persistent invitation to seek and do the will of God in one's life. I rejected the heavy judgment and fear of YFC rallies, though they got me to thinking about, imagining my life as a Christian. The will of God for my life, I could get. The will-of-God emphasis freed me to make public my strong teenage leaning toward ministry as a life calling. The positive from, in spite of the negative.

Poetry and imagination. I could move inside this beckoning song. I could move beyond God up there to God in here and make a life fired by imagination. I really could be a preacher. Linda and I really could launch a life together. I could find a way to go to seminary and then earn the coveted doctorate. We both could produce books. I could write speeches for President and Mrs. Jimmy Carter and then become part of the White House staff. I could work for religious liberty. We could raise a great family. We could overcome our share of bad choices, health and emotional challenges. Poetic flair could ignite our imagination to lead a splendid but declining congregation to partner with a neighbor church, creating the beautiful and strong out of the two. The fifty-year-old Baptist church could reinvent itself into a vibrant faith and action center that blesses a host of people literally around the world.

When I stand on my tiptoes and add all this up, I can readily say that I am a Jesus person with confidence in a relationship with Jesus of Galilee as well as Jesus of the twenty-first century. Since meeting Jesus of Nazareth, I have sought to shape my active ministry, my faithing praxis, in ways I determined to reflect what Jesus daily did among the people of Galilee. I can shape a daily ministry in the shadow of Jesus of Nazareth, fueled by a growing existential experience with the ever-living Jesus, beyond his own history. I am coming to see that, as a Jesus person, I can move beyond the often demeaning theological squab-bles that undercut effective service in Jesus' name. Hearing echoes of Jesus in Matthew 25, feeding the hungry, clothing the naked, caring for the sick and incarcerated puts me on a new footing with people of all faiths and no visible faith who likewise move among the least of these. Ambiguities abound that serve to keep me on this faithing journey, a trek with no boundaries and no discernible destination.

On the drumbeat of poetically energized imagination continues persuad-ing millions to dream of a better way. Robert Kennedy said it well: "There are those that look at things the way they are, and ask why? I dream of things that never were, and ask why not?" I like that. At eighty, by the grace of God, in the love of Linda, encouraged by great friends, I continue to ask, "Why not?"

I conclude with a moving poem that gathers up both the poetry and imagination of my faithing at eighty. It comes from the mind and heart of two of my favorite people: Rev. Tim Tutt preached the sermon on "Light" at Westmoreland Congregational United Church of Christ, Bethesda, Maryland. Dr. Bill Rogers, retired professor and ever-vital sage living in Charlotte, North Carolina, using his fertile imagination, translated the sermon into poetry.

In the very beginning of time itself…
This Little Light I Am
By Timothy B. Tutt and William B. Rogers

Something like 14 billion years ago…
Creation breathed an explosive note of hope into being
And the universe was begun…
Time began to unfold.

In that creative and miraculous instant,
the simplest of elements,
began to pour forth into the universe,
like a never-ending number of clowns
piling out of a tiny car at the circus.
spilled everywhere into space.

And in the beautiful darkness of early time,
the life-shaping force of gravity
began to work with the atoms that were all around.
Like a skilled mason placing bricks just so in a wall.
Or like a potter shaping clay on a spinning wheel,
Gravity began to pull the atoms together,
Melding it tighter and tighter,
so tight that, finally,
the simple atoms couldn't help themselves…
And with cosmic fertility
they doubled their protons and created a new helium atom,
almost like parents drawn together in love creating new children.

And the power of those atoms
was so strong in their coming together

that something new was born in the universe:
Light…
Light we know as stars,
winking at us in the night sky,
giant balls clinging so tightly to each other
that their power made yet another element:
Helium.

All the while
gravity was squeezing the elements of the stars together—
Maybe it helps to think of gravity as a cook in the kitchen kneading
    dough,
consistently making the dough thicker—
With gravity working so diligently,
the elements of the stars became so heavy
there was nothing left for the stars to do except to explode
with an uncertain pregnancy.

Some of the stars burst with titanic explosions,
filled with the potential of new life
that transcended their brilliant deaths.

As they died,
these stars sent leftover dust into the cosmos.
And at various places,
drawn together with a sort of longing for communion,
some of the dust of old stars was gathered up
by the gravitational pull of new stars,
and the star dust formed planets around the stars.
And we call those new planets solar systems.

And that is where we come in:
About four and half billion years ago,
our planet coalesced,
formed from the dust of older stars.
Our planet,
flying around this great ball of light called the sun,

is, at the same time,
the byproduct of other lights, long gone.

You could say,
in astronomical ways,
that we are the product of light.
You could say,
in biological ways,
that we are the children of the stars.
You could say,
in evolutionary language,
that we are the product of this great cosmic energy,
this creative unfolding of the universe.
You could say,
in the poetic language of theology,
that we are the light of the world,
a city set on a hill.

In the fullness of time,
the stardust of this planet earth moved and molded—
Again it may help to think of the work creation as an artist…
Maybe a ceramics artist working with clay and water and fire.
Or maybe a blacksmith intent upon her crafting—
And the water and warmth of our planet earth reached
just the right mix
for cells to
bubble up
out of the ocean.
And one day,
one of those bubbling cells emerged
that could turn the energy of sunlight into chemical energy.
And the ability to turn sunlight into chemical energy
became part of the first plants.
And all around, the cells changed and flourished
until one day,
a day whose exact date is lost in the mist of memory,

but one grand day,
A human stood upon the earth—
a human like you and me—
a human connected through
billions and billions of years
back to sunlight
and stardust
and gravity
and energy.
The other truth is that the dust we are is the dust of stars,
light years upon light years away.
From light we came,
to light we belong.
Neuroscience can't yet tell us this is true,
but I think the reptilian brain,
the oldest part of the human brain,
remembers in some visceral way
our ancient origins.
So many of the world's religious rituals involve water—
Hindus bathing in the Ganges,
a Buddhist water libation ritual,
Muslims washing before prayer,
the Christian celebration of baptism.
I think water is important to us
because we remember, in some way beyond words,
that moment when we as living organisms
emerged from the water.
And I think we understand ourselves as light
and we understand God as light
because somewhere in the deepest parts of our brains
we remember that we belong to light,
that we are created from the dust of light.

This little light...I am.

The God of creation as remembered in the opening lines of Genesis said, "Let there be light." At eighty I celebrate that light, creation's light, light from distant stars, and light from Linda, Tim, Bill, and that great host of witnesses. That light continues its grand, cosmic, immanent, collective unconsciousness, generative, illumination to me. I embrace that light and pray I will reflect that light to others until my own light dims and goes out. Selah.

ENDNOTES

[1] C. P. Cavafy.

[2] Anderson Cooper and Gloria Vanderbilt, *The Rainbow Comes and Goes: A Mother and Son on Life, Love, and Loss* (New York: Harper & Row, 2014), 192.

[3] Barbara Brown Taylor, *The Preaching Life* (Cambridge: Cowley Publishers, 1993), 11.

[4] Wilfred Cantwell Smith, *The Meaning and End of Religion* (Minneapolis: Fortress Press, 1991), 181.

[5] Christian Wiman, *My Bright Abyss: Meditation of a Modern Believer* (New York: Farrar, Straus and Giroux, 2013), 17–18.

[6] Smith, 181.

[7] Marcus Borg, *Meeting Jesus Again for the First Time: The Historical Jesus and the Heart of Contemporary Faith* (New York: HarperCollins, 1992), 88.

[8] The pronunciation of Vienna, Georgia, comes down hard on the "i" rather than "e."

[9] John Shelby Spong, *Why Christianity Must Change or Die: A Bishop Speaks to Believers in Exile.*

[10] Smith, 156.

[11] Ibid., 172.

[12] Wiman, x.

[13] Sepphoris is never mentioned in any of the four narratives about Jesus or Paul's writings, though the city dominated much of the life of that part of Galilee.

[14] Borg, summary from several passages of *Meeting Jesus Again for the First Time.*

PARTIAL (REMEMBERED) BIBLIOGRAPHY

Armstrong, Karen. *The Battle For God: A History of Fundamentalism*. New York: Random House, 2000.

_____*The Bible A Biography*. New York: Atlantic Monthly Press, 2007.

_____Numerous lectures

Bass, Diana Butler. *Grounded: Finding God in the World—A Spiritual Revolution*. New York: HarperOne, 2015.

_____*A People's History of Christianity: The Other Side of the Story*. New York: HarperCollins, 2013.

_____*Christianity For the Rest Of Us*. New York: HarperCollins, 2006.

_____Lectures and personal conversations.

Beal, Timothy. *The Rise and Fall of the Bible: The Unexpected History of an Accidental Book*. New York: Houghton, Mifflin, Harcourt, 2011.

_____Lecture and personal conversation

Bonhoeffer, Dietrich. *The Cost of Discipleship*. New York: Macmillan, 1937.

Borg, Marcus. *Jesus and Buddha: The Parallel Sayings*. Berkeley: Ulysses Press, 1997.

_____*Meeting Jesus Again for the First Time: The Historical Jesus and Heart of Contemporary Christianity*. New York: HarperCollins, 1992.

_____*Reading The Bible Again for the First Time: Taking the Bible Seriously but not Literally*. New York: HarperCollins,

_____Numerous lectures, tapes, visit with President Jimmy Carter and personal conversations

Borg, Marcus and John Dominic Crossan. *The First Christmas: What the Gospels Really Teach About Jesus' Birth*. New York: HarperOne, 1989.

_____*The First Paul: Reclaiming the Radical Visionary Behind the Church's Conservative Icon*. New York: HarperOne, 2009.

_____*The Last Week: What the Gospels Really Teach About Jesus' Final Days in Jerusalem*. New York: HarperSanFrancisco, 2006.

_____Numerous lectures, recordings and personal conversations.

Brown, Raymond. *The Birth of the Messiah: A Commentary on the Infancy Narratives in the Gospels of Matthew and Luke*. New York: Doubleday, 1998.

_____*The Death of the Messiah, from Gethsemane to the Grave: A Commentary on the Passion Narratives in the Four Gospels*, Vol. 1 & 2. New York: Doubleday, 1994.

Carter, Jimmy. *Faith, A Journey For All*. New York: Simon and Schuster, 2018

_____Numerous lectures, presentations, small group and personal conversations.

Cooper, Anderson and Gloria Vanderbilt. *The Rainbow Comes and Goes*. New York: Harper & Row, 2014.

Crossan, John Dominic. T*he Birth of Christianity: Discovering What Happened in the Years Immediately After the Execution of Jesus*. New York: San Francisco, 1998.

_____*The Greatest Prayer: Rediscovering the Revolutionary Message of the Lord's Prayer*. New York: HarperOne, 2010.

_____*A Long Way From Tipperary: What a Former Monk Discovered in His Search for Truth*. New York: HarperSanFrancisco, 2000.

_____*Who Killed Jesus: Exposing the Roots of Anti-Semitism in the Gospel Story of the Death of Jesus*. New York: HarperSanFrancisco, 1995.

_____*Jesus: A Revolutionary Biography*. New York: HarperSanFrancisco, 1994.

_____Numerous lectures and recordings

Cupitt, Don. *Above You Only Sky*. Santa Rosa: Polebridge Press, 2008.

_____*The Sea of Faith*. New York: Cambridge University Press, 1998.

_____*Taking Leave of God*. London: SCM Press, 1979.

_____Lectures and recordings.

De Chardin. Pierre Teilhard. *The Phenomenon of Man*. New York: Harper & Ros, 1955.

_____*The Divine Milieu*. New York: Harper & Row, 1960.

Eagleman, David. *Incognito: The Secret Lives of the Brain*. New York: Pantheon, 2011.

_____*Sum: Forty Tales from the Afterlife*. New York: Knopf, 2010.

Fosdick, Harry Emerson. *The Living of These Days*. New York: Harper, 1956.

Funk, Robert W. *Honest to Jesus: Jesus for a New Millennium*. New York: Harper & Row, 1996

_____*Language, Hermeneutic and Word of God*. New York: Harper & Row, 1966.

_____Lectures, recordings and one memorable personal conversation.

Geering, Lloyd. *Christian Faith at the Crossroads: A Map of Modern Religions*. Santa Rosa: Polebridge Press, 2001.

_____*Coming Back to Earth*. Salem: Polebridge Press, 2009.

_____*The World to Come: From Christian Past to Global Future*. Santa Rosa: Polebridge Press, 1999.

_____Lectures and recordings.

Jung, C.G. *Memories, Dreams Reflections*. New York: Random House, 1961.

Leaves, Nigel. *Odyssey on the Sea of Faith: The Life & Writings of Don Cupitt*. Santa Rosa: Polebridge Press, 2004.

Ludemann, Gerd. *The Resurrection of Christ: A Historical Inquiry*. Amherst: Prometheus Books, 2004.

Marney, Carlyle. *Priests to Each Other*. Macon: Smyth & Helwys, 1974.

_____Limited but memorable personal conversation.

Meier, John. *A Marginal Jew: Rethinking the Historical Jesus*. New York: Doubleday, 1991.

Nouwen, Henri. *The Wounded Healer: Ministry in Contemporary Society*. New York: Image Books, 1979.

Nussbaum, Martha C. *Upheavals of Thought: The Intelligence of Emotions*. New York: Cambridge University Press, 2001.

O'Connor, Elizabeth. *Call to Commitment*. New York: Harper & Row, 1963.

_____*Journey Inward, Journey Outward*. New York: Harper & Row, 1968.

Pagels, Elaine. *Adam, Eve, and the Serpent*. New York: Random House, 1988.

_____*The Gnostic Gospels*. New York: Random House, 2004.

_____*The Origin of Satan*. New York: Random House, 1995.

_____Numerous lectures and limited personal conversations.

Robinson, John A.T. *Honest to God*. London: SCM Press, 1963.

Sanford, E.P. *The Kingdom Within: The Inner Meanings of Jesus' Sayings*. New York: HarperOne, 1987.

Scott, Bernard Brandon. *Hear Then the Parables: A Commentary on the Parables of Jesus*. Minneapolis: Fortress Press, 1989.

_____Numerous lectures and limited personal conversations.

Shlain, Leonard. *The Alphabet Versus the Goddess: The Conflict Between*. New York: Penguin Press, 1998.

Smith, Wilfred Cantwell. *The Meaning and End of Religion*. Minneapolis: Fortress Press, 1991.

Spong, John Shelby. *Born of a Woman: A Bishop Rethinks the Virgin Birth in a Male-Dominated Church*. New York: HarperSanFrancisco, 1992.

_____*Here I Stand: My Struggle for a Christianity of Integrity, Love, and Equality*. New York: HarperSanFrancisco, 2000.

_____*Why Christianity Must Change or Die*. New York: HarperSanFrancisco, 2001.

_____*Liberating the Gospels: Reading the Bible With Jewish Eyes*. New York: HarperSanFrancisco, 1996.

_____Numerous lectures, recordings and limited personal conversations.

Taylor, Barbara Brown. *The Preaching Life*. Washington: Cowley Publications, 1993.

Whitman, Walt. *Leaves of Grass*. Brooklyn, 1885.

Wiman, Christian. *My Bright Abyss: Meditation of a Modern Believer*. New York: Farrar, Straus and Giroux, 2013.

_____Lectures and personal conversations.

About the Author

Born in Atlanta, 1937, Robert L. Maddox, Jr. is eldest of four sons born to Robert and Virginia Maddox of Atlanta. He is a graduate of Clarkston High School, Clarkston, GA, Baylor University, Waco; Southwestern Theological Seminary, Fort Worth, Texas; Doctor of Sacred Theology, Candler School of Theology, Emory University, Atlanta. He was ordained as a Southern Baptist minister in 1963, and became a United Church of Christ minister in 2006. In addition to church staff positions, he served as pastor of First Baptist Church, Vienna, GA; First Baptist Church, Calhoun, GA; Mayfield Road Baptist Church, Arlington, TX; Briggs Memorial Baptist Church, Bethesda, MD; and Minister of Discipleship and Interim Senior Pastor, Westmoreland Congregational United Church of Christ, Bethesda.

Currently, he is the Executive Director, Briggs Center for Faith and Action, Bethesda, an organization founded by Robert Maddox that grew out of the former Briggs Church. He is adjunct professor at Wesley Theological Seminary, Washington, DC, for student pastors.

Maddox was a speechwriter and religious liaison with President Jimmy Carter at the White House, and has an ongoing relationship with President and Mrs. Carter.

He served as Assistant to the president, Pitt Community College, Greenville, SC; Executive Director, Americans United for Separation of Church and State.; and Editor, *Capital Baptist*, District of Columbia Baptist Convention, Washington, DC.

He is author of *Preacher at the White House; Acts, Layman's Bible Book Commentary; Separation of Church and State: Guarantor of Religious Freedom; Prostate Cancer: What I Found Out & What You Should Know*. In addition he wrote eight Bible studies for the Southern Baptist Sunday School, numerous articles, and editorials.

Maddox was Chairman of the board, Interfaith Conference, Metropolitan Washington, DC.

He has been married to Linda Cook of Thomaston, GA, since 1959. Together, they have three children and five grandchildren.

RECOMMENDATIONS

Reflecting and re-imagining the religious story at the center of his life, Robert Maddox embodies a probing, restless seeker. (I have witnessed his journey for more than sixty years.) Rather than clinging to one view, he asks the readers to open ourselves to other views and entertain multiple possibilities.

—Dr. William B. Rogers,
Distinguished Professor of Religious Education (Retired),
philosopher, author, blogger and poet,
Charlotte, North Carolina

This wide-ranging book, tracing Bob Maddox's spiritual journey — what he calls 'faithing' — over the course of eight decades spoke to me. I resonated with his descriptions of growing up in the Southern Baptist tradition with its marvelous hymns, its invitations to come to Jesus, its profound certainty and its racism. Reading this felt like a crash course in Biblical history, in theology as poetry, in the historical Jesus seminar, and in the many people in Bob's life who shaped his faith journey as a 'Jesus person.' Most of all, I was inspired by his continued searching, his voracious curiosity, and his openness to change as he was shaped by the 'ever-unfolding cumulative Christian tradition.' I hope that when I'm 80 years old, I'll be half as insightful and curious as Bob reveals himself to be in this book.

—Dr. Elizabeth Ferris,
Georgetown University, Washington, DC;
scholar, author, and world acclaimed advocate for
displaced persons, especially women

In *A Faith Journey: No Boundaries; No Conclusions* Bob Maddox has written a graceful personal memoir that is also a powerful communal story. It is a telling of his faithing journey; it is a larger narrative of the nation. His book is both an individual confession and a collective call to action.

—Rev. Timothy B. Tutt,
Senior Minister, Westmoreland Congregational United Church of Christ,
Bethesda, Maryland

Rev. Bob Maddox's memoir is a reflective piece of his own personal faith journey and its connection with larger trends in the Christian movement. Persuasive, intellectual, and easy to keep reading, is a book I would absolutely recommend especially for young people, like me, starting out on their own faith journey. This book helps me understand why Rev. Maddox takes the positions he does and had me doing some serious introspection as it addressed larger questions about our relationship with God and Jesus.

—Andrew Hallward-Driemeier,
honors student, Williams College, Williamstown, Massachusetts